Writers and Personality

Also by Louis Auchincloss

Writers and Personality

Louis Auchincloss

University of South Carolina Press

© 2005 University of South Carolina

Published in Columbia, South Carolina,
by the University of South Carolina Press

Manufactured in the United States of America

09 08 07 06 05 5 4 3 2 1

Library of Congress Cataloging-in-Publication Data

Auchincloss, Louis.
  Writers and personality / Louis Auchincloss.
    p. cm.
  ISBN 1-57003-580-6 (cloth : alk. paper)
  1. Authorship—Psychological aspects. 2. Authors—Psychology. I. Title.
  PN171.P83A83 2005
  809—dc22

                                                        2004030832

For Susan Henshaw Jones, director and president of the Museum of the City of New York

Contents

Writers and Personality

Proem

SAM A. LEWISOHN, the great art collector, wrote a book entitled *Painters and Personality,* in the foreword to which he wrote: "In the creation of significant art the personality of the artist is the decisive factor." I am not sure that this is strictly true of writers of fiction, with whom this little book will be concerned. Flaubert, after all, believed that a novelist should keep himself entirely out of his story. But perhaps the very suppression of a personality may be an aspect of it. Don't we have a sense of Flaubert in *Madame Bovary,* lurking behind the pages? At any rate, Lewisohn got me thinking on the subject, and these essays are the result of my ruminations.

The Brontës

HENRY JAMES EXPRESSED what many readers have comfortably —and some uncomfortably—felt about the strong and seemingly unbreakable ties between the lives of the three Brontë sisters and their novels. As he put it:

> The romantic tradition of the Brontës, with posterity, has been still more essentially helped, I think, by a force independent of any one of their applied faculties—by the attendant image of their dreary, their tragic history, their loneliness and poverty of life. That picture has been made to hang before us as insistently as the vividest page of *Jane Eyre* or *Wuthering Heights*. If these things were "stories," as we say, and stories of a lively interest, the medium from which they sprang was above all else in itself a story, such a story as fairly elbowed out the rights of appreciation, as has come at last to impose itself as an expression of the power concerned.

It almost seems as if the sombre and touching picture of those three young women of weak lungs, dwelling in a grim parsonage surrounded by graves and bleak moors and scribbling out their flaming stories in tiny letters on precious sheets of foolscap, was a somehow essential background to a full appreciation of their fiction. I know that my own visit to Haworth Parsonage was a far more moving experience than any I encountered at other authors' shrines, with the sole exception of Emily Dickinson's in Amherst. But James may be making the point, though he does not stress it, that the association of the home with the works may in part excuse the latter from attaining the first literary rank. He tended to overlook the Brontës in his extended review of Victorian fiction, though we know that he revered Emily as a poet and read aloud her "Cold in the earth" with effective solemnity to Edith Wharton's houseguests. But I do put *Jane Eyre, Villette,* and *Wuthering Heights* in the first literary rank, and I find their biographical background an intrinsic part of their writers' personalities. It would be there if we knew nothing at all about their private lives.

Their father, the Reverend Patrick Brontë, a widower from their earliest years, was a devout and stern minister of a church, totally convinced of the rich rewards and terrible punishments of an afterlife far more important than the one given us, but he was also a kindly if not always understanding parent and a man of sometimes amiable and sometimes alarming eccentricities. But to me the important aspect of his personality was that of an enthusiastic if unendowed romantic poet. The father who wrote this verse could not have been totally uncongenial with his gifted daughters.

> Ye feathered songsters of the grove,
> Sweet Philomel and cooing dove,
> Goldfinch and linnet gray,
> And mellow thrush and blackbird loud,
> And lark, shrill warbler of the crowd,
> Where do you pensive stray?

Winifred Guerin has written that Anne Brontë was the first of the sisters to point the way to fiction of bare and simple realism in her representation of the life of an underpaid and overworked governess for an arrogant and demanding family in *Agnes Grey*. The novel is certainly not what George Moore called it—"the most perfect prose narrative in English literature"— but it has a modest charm of its own without arousing any of the excitement of her sisters' big novels. What must have impressed the sisters when they read aloud to each other from works in progress was the drastic contrast it offered to the kind of thing all three had been previously scribbling: the monstrous loves, hates, and massacres of the imaginary kingdoms of Gondal and Angria.

Of course, they were living in the age of Byron and the extravaganzas of the free soul, and it is easy to imagine the release from the dreary monotony of Haworth that such poems as "The Corsair" and "Lara" brought to young women whose only hope for romance lay in marriage to one of the local curates later pilloried by Charlotte in *Shirley*. Wandering as they did on the moors, and presented with the drama of stormy weather over the barren and far-stretching landscape, they were able to supplement their reading of Byron and Scott with a sense that their souls were no longer confined to the dark stone houses and cobbled streets of their native village but free to blend with the wildness of nature and seeming infinity.

[4]

But they never lost sight of that native village. There was an *Agnes Grey* in all three of them. It was what qualified their Byronicism. The author of "Lara" had a sentimental side that induced him to emphasize the human and caring nature of his corsair. As a pirate he might have slain untold numbers of hapless sailors, but at home he showed generosity:

> Cool to the great, contemptuous to the high,
> The humble passed not his unheeding eye,
> Much he would speak not, but beneath his roof
> They found asylum oft, and ne'er reproof.

Still, a lofty pride, as with his literary creator, was the dominant aspect of the corsair's personality.

> What cared he for the freedom of the crowd?
> He raised the humble but to bend the proud.

Charlotte seems to echo something of this in her arrogant characters, as when Blanche Ingram in *Jane Eyre* addresses a footman: "Cease thy chatter, block-head, and do my bidding!"

Charlotte and Anne, however, were not more concerned with bending the proud than raising the humble; their philanthropy was perfectly sincere and genuine, and if they admired the dash and courage of some of the savage characters in their juvenilia I do not think they were ever deluded into condoning their evil. With Emily this may be subject to some qualification. She and Byron may not be too far apart in these lines from "Manfred":

> The mind which is immortal makes itself
> Requital for its good or evil thoughts—
> Is its own origin in ill and end—
> And its own place and time—its innate sense,
> When stripped of this mortality derives
> No color from the fleeting things without,
> But is absorbed in sufferance or in joy,
> Born from the knowledge of its own desert.

Here we come close, I believe, to Emily's conception of Heathcliff. Totally amoral, he feels responsible to nobody but himself for the hideous wrongs he inflicts on persons who have done him no earthly harm. Edgar, Isabella, and Catherine Linton, Hareton Hinshaw, and even Heathcliff's own son must suffer for the wrong done Heathcliff by Hindley Earnshaw. It is not enough that the last named is thoroughly and deservedly crushed. All Lintons and Earnshaws must pay for his maltreatment of his father's ward.

Heathcliff's sex appeal, largely attributed to him by readers eager to find it, has blurred Emily's more graphic portrait. Laurence Olivier's romantic portrayal of him in the film with Merle Oberon did much to keep alive the twisted vision. But what is Heathcliff, really? Perhaps, like the white whale in *Moby Dick,* he is anything the reader wants in the way of evil, something sent from infernal regions, or simply the presence in the world of an opposite to creative force, a negative to a positive, a war to a peace, a stormy winter to a benign spring. But it is always clear to me that Emily, like her narrating housekeeper, Nelly Dean, has a certain sympathy for him.

Of course, Heathcliff is wronged as a boy, savagely wronged by his adoptive father's son who treats him as a kind of household slave. But it is not by any means only for this that he wreaks his fearful revenge on everybody connected with Hindley Earnshaw. It is because he overhears Hindley's sister Cathy telling Nelly Dean that a marriage to himself would disgrace her and because she married Edgar Linton that he feels compelled to tear the world apart. And in the end of her novel Emily seems to be telling us that he is redeemed by his passion for Cathy and that death will translate them both into a kind of beneficent union with the spirit of the moors.

Now what is all that by way of a philosophy? To some readers it might seem that Emily is promoting a theory that a man who has spent his life degrading his fellow creatures to misery, poverty, and ignorance can be totally redeemed by his violent attachment to a married woman whom he cannot abstain from harassing, and will be ultimately rewarded with a blissful after life. Is that a creed to sustain one?

Of course, the answer is that we needn't stray beyond the limits of the story itself. *Wuthering Heights* is simply a great novel, the result of the perfect fusion of its author's passionately imaginative personality and her superb narrative skill.

There is a tendency among Brontë enthusiasts to clothe the person of Emily in the robes of fiery independence and isolation suggested by her novel, to see her as aloof, proud, her face directed at the wind and storm of the moors, and there *was* something of that in her. But she was also a person determined to take her part in the humblest household chores, to prepare herself, however reluctantly, to be a teacher and contribute to the family income, and she joined with her sisters in their efforts to get their fiction published. She suffered as they did from unfavorable reviews, and she was at work on a second novel, the manuscript of which she may have destroyed, shortly before she died. She was also the one great poet of the family, and I think she knew it. In other words, for all her moor wanderings and sky gazing, she was a dedicated professional artist who sought above all things to give tangible expression to her imagination.

And that she certainly succeeded in doing. She had none of her sisters' didacticism; the moral improvement of her fellow beings was never her concern. She wanted to tell the story of what happened when the father of Cathy Earnshaw brought back from a trip to Liverpool the dark little bundle of satanic mischief that he had rescued from starvation in the streets. Where had Heathcliff come from? How did he make his money in the period of his absence from Wuthering Heights? Would a man capable of such fiendish cruelty be capable of so annihilating a passion for a woman? But are we even much interested in the answers to such questions? The story grips us to the exclusion of other considerations, and we finish it with a sense of awe. We can make anything we want of it; all we know is that it remains with us— we have been caught up in Emily's extraordinary personality. That, I must suppose, is great art.

Nothing is more often said about Charlotte than that her fiction exposed to the British reading public what had long been kept more or less under the hat: that women are subject to the same sexual passions as men. I am not going to gainsay this: the feeling of Jane Eyre for Mr. Rochester, of Lucy Snowe for Professor Emanuel, of Caroline Helstone for Robert Moore, certainly struck a chord in English letters that had been only lightly touched before. Nor do I wish to deny that such passions were an essential aspect of Charlotte's own very vivid personality, as her many misery-wracked letters to Constantin Heger confirm. The point I wish to make is that the aspect of Charlotte's personality that contributed most to the enduring popularity of her work was the strongly felt presence in almost every page of a plain, brave, but relentless little woman, never in the least abashed by rank, wealth, or power, whose crystal clear stare takes in every nook and cranny of an often disorderly world and subjects everyone, including herself, and not excepting those in the grip of passion, to the stern moral judgment of a Victorian code. The journals of the Queen herself, candid, straight-to-the-point, literal, at times severe, at times naive, highly personal, never dull, have something of the same quality. And Victoria loved *Jane Eyre*.

For Charlotte *is* Jane Eyre and Lucy Snowe. Our pleasure in her characterizations is drawn from the absolute honesty of her own revelations; it intensifies our identification with her heroines. We admire the courage and lack of self-pity with which they face adversity, and we come to share their optimism that enough determination and character should get them over their hurdles in the absence of too long a run of bad luck. In *Villette* Charlotte goes so far as to allow her own experience to end the novel tragically. As in life her passion for the married Professor Heger could have no fruition, so in her book Lucy could not wed Paul Emanuel, who had to be lost in a storm at sea. Of course, Emanuel was not married, but as he was Heger to the life, Charlotte could not give herself even fictionally to him.

In the novel in which Charlotte chose not to use an "I" character to narrate her tale, but to make herself the omniscient author, *Shirley,* her personality is present, for the most part, only in the sections in which she expresses a point of view on the action, and its absence in the other sections is fatal to the interest. This novel, in the absence of the greater two, would not have made an enduring name for Charlotte. *Shirley* is mostly interesting as a study of Charlotte's misunderstanding of her own literary powers.

She set out to write a book about the rights and wrongs involved in the riots of the textile workers in northern England caused by the introduction of labor-saving machinery—an example of the didacticism to which she and Anne were sadly prone—but she didn't find the riots adequate material to base a whole novel on, so she introduced a satire on curates, a handful of irrelevant character studies, and, finally, a curiously unconvincing picture of how her sister Emily might have developed had she been born an heiress in good health. The novel, anyway, is a dull hodge-podge, including a young girl's death thrown into the mix, and the reader sadly misses a Lucy Snowe or a Jane Eyre.

Yet there is passion in *Shirley,* though it may be a strong word to describe what Caroline Helstone and Shirley Keeldar feel for Robert and Louis Moore, respectively. Yet Caroline almost dies of the humiliation of unrequited love—a lady should not cast her affections where they are not returned—and when, in the end, Robert marries her largely out of pity, we are a long way from the stormy finale of *Villette* or the radiantly happy one of *Jane Eyre.*

Anne Brontë had a personality more subdued and gentler than that of her elder sisters. This did not mean, however, that she was meek or easily put upon; on the contrary, her record as a governess in two arrogant and demanding families shows a considerable amount of stamina, and Charlotte recounted touchingly the brave spirit in which she faced her extinction. But being the youngest of Patrick's children she was the most exposed to the stern religious teaching of the Wesleyan Miss Branwell, the maternal maiden aunt who came to take the place of the mother she never knew, and, more so than her siblings, she imbibed the gloomy faith that fastened one's thoughts on heaven and hell at the expense of the here and now. Anne's religiosity seemed to grow, even after her aunt's death, and when she came to write *The Tenant of Wildfell Hall* she allowed a personality, drenched in moral instruction, to pervade too many of its chapters. Indeed, she makes no secret of the fact that, in writing the novel, she was fulfilling her Christian duty of warning her readers of the life- and soul-destroying effects of alcoholism.

The example, of course, which set her on her mission was her brother Branwell, who died wretchedly of drink and drugs after a woefully mismanaged life, leaving a few writings that offer no evidence of the genius with which some of his contemporaries sought to endow him.

It is a pity, for not only did Anne's faith weigh down her novel; it probably never kept a reader from another drink. But *The Tenant of Wildfell Hall* shows plenty of evidence that Anne was endowed with a narrative skill approaching that of her sisters, and that if more of the personality hidden under the evangelical layer had been allowed to emerge she might have been almost their equal.

The novel, like *Wuthering Heights,* is divided into two narratives: a man's and a woman's. There may be some initial puzzlement to a reader as to why either narrator should be at such pains to record his or her observations at quite such length or in quite such detail, relating conversations that could never be so clearly recalled, but once one has surrendered to the grip of the story, this artificiality is soon forgotten.

The first narrator is Gilbert Markham, a handsome and virile young gentleman farmer, the cock of the walk in his small neighborhood, adored by his widowed mother, efficient in managing his crops and livestock, flirting with the local girls whom his mother considers beneath him, dominating a sassy kid brother, and living for the cheerful moment. His growing and ultimately passionate attraction to a mysterious and beautiful widow—or seeming widow —who has rented a broken-down manor house for herself and her small son, and his stormy repudiation of the insidious rumors about her past that spring up in the community, deepen his character and turn him into a serious man. Soon he is willing to take on the whole neighborhood in her defense, and when he discovers—or thinks he has discovered—that there may be truth in the stories about her, he thrashes and almost kills the man he thinks to be her lover. Neither Charlotte nor Emily did a more forcible or convincing study of a young male.

The seeming widow, Helen, now submits her diary to Gilbert, whom she has come to love, to clear her name, and these pages constitute most of the balance of the novel. The diary reveals the horror of her marriage to a violent alcoholic and her humiliation before the riotous behavior of his male houseguests. Anne Brontë does not pull her punches here. She makes it clear that Helen actually comes to hate the spouse from whom at last she has to flee when he induces her little boy to drink, but she returns when he is dying of his own excesses to nurse him and guide his soul to redemption. In the end, of course, she is free to marry Gilbert. There was no Heger that we know of in Anne's life. I dare to think that with a red pencil to eliminate the fulsomely religious sections I could almost turn the book into a best seller.

Gustave Flaubert

USTAVE FLAUBERT, deemed by many literary critics the ultimate novelist, the craftsman who carried the art to its greatest perfection in *Madame Bovary,* believed in keeping his own personality rigidly separate from his work, so that the latter should stand apart with an independence all of its own.

He shows Emma Bovary for exactly what she is, without pity, blame, or excuse, without partiality or hostility, as if she were some protozoan placed under the microscope of a scientist interested in truth at the cost of any previous conception of it. She is endowed with a moderate intelligence and a roaming imagination, married to a kindly but dull and inept physician, and isolated in a small village of mean-minded shopkeepers and artisans. In short, she is placed in the position, neither better nor worse, of untold thousands of French middle-class women of her era. There is no suggestion that the disaster which overtakes her is the expected or even deserved fate of such. No, this is Emma Bovary, *her* story, and if what happens to her gives rise to a host of speculations, well, that is the reader's affair.

It is Emma's imagination that does her in. She is the victim of all the slushy romanticism with which the unfortunate seek to alleviate the tedium of their lives: daydreaming of God and his angels awaiting the good, of the delights of distant Paris, of white knights rescuing lonely and desolate females. Emma finds only the reflection of her own ego in her visions of heaven, only bankruptcy in her purchase of expensive trumpery to make her home more like one in the nation's capital, and only desertion in the two lovers she takes for white knights. Her final solution is to swallow arsenic, leaving her husband to disillusionment and an early death and her little daughter to the bitter hands of charity.

It is natural to ask if Emma's creator doesn't have some message for us. Might he be suggesting that Emma is the sorry victim of an over-commercialized, money-minded, and bigoted culture? Or that people shouldn't live in small towns? Or that we should keep slushy literature from our children? Or even that a woman should be raised with an objective other than finding a husband? But I think Flaubert's purpose is more like that of Willa Cather when she wrote *My Antonia*. Elizabeth Sergeant has related how Cather set an old Sicilian apothecary jar, filled with orange-brown flowers, in the middle of a bare round antique table and said: "I want my new heroine to be like this— like a rare object in the middle of a table, which one may examine from all sides."

It would seem then that Flaubert has succeeded in suppressing all evidence of his personality. And yet some of it seeps gratifyingly through. The man who is so intensely conscious of all the cheats of a self-advertising civilization and the daydreaming which it engenders to keep the masses chained in the kind of half life that Emma leads, emerges from time to time in his mordant humor and compassion for the dumb and easily led.

In the public meeting of the Agricultural Committee in Yonville, attended by Emma and her soon-to-be first lover, a silver medal is awarded to one Catherine Leroux for fifty-four years of service at the same farm. The poor shabby, ignorant, and illiterate old woman, who has been so long associated with farm animals as to have taken on some of their mutism and placidity, is too bewildered by the noise and crowd to know what is going on and has to be pushed to the dais. *"Qu'elle est bête!"* is the cry. But when she sees the medal a beatific smile suffuses her countenance and she murmurs that she will give it to her local priest so that he may say a mass for her. *"Quel fanatisme!"* mutters the free-thinking pharmacist Homais.

I feel it is Flaubert himself who comments: "A half century of servitude confronted the gaping burghers." As I am sure it is the author himself who writes the final sentence of the novel about Homais who has cheated everyone in town: "He has just received the *croix d'honneur.*"

There is also something of Flaubert's own innate romanticism in Emma Bovary's daydreaming. It was something that he sternly checked when he was writing about contemporary France, as in *Madame Bovary* and *L'Education sentimentale,* but to which he could give freer vent when he drew the more allowably exotic scenes of ancient Carthage in *Salambô,* or Palestine in *Herodias.* He fully saw the dangers of fantasizing in his portraits of Emma and Frédéric Moreau; it was a dangerous habit that had to be converted in himself to a useful and perhaps even indispensable tool in reconstructing the long lost worlds of Hamilcar Barca and Herod Antipas.

Flaubert might have apologized for even the slimmest glimpse of his own personality in *Madame Bovary*, but I find it reassuring to have the occasional sense that its humanitarian author is just as appalled by what is taking place as I am. And I miss it in the later works, in which he withdraws altogether.

The Carthage of *Salambô,* whose unpaid mercenaries revolt and are annihilated, is about as far from Yonville as one can get, and it was not difficult for its author to remove himself altogether from its arcane and bloody settings and its operatic plot. As a combination of tireless research and vividly descriptive writing it is indeed a remarkable work, but I am content to salute it as an artistic tour de force and let it go at that. My principal reaction to all its gore and thunder is to be thankful that I wasn't born in Carthage in the aftermath of the first Punic War.

L'Education sentimentale was written many years after Flaubert's first two novels, and obviously after long consideration and preparation, so it is natural for a reader to ask once again what he is supposed to make of its theme and thesis. Is there a thesis? Why does he write a long novel about the France of the last years of the reign of Louis Philippe and offer as our principal perceiving eye a silly ass? For Frédéric Moreau is a young man, devoid of any real ambition, mildly epicurean, wholly selfish and egotistical, who squanders his money, neglects his mother, deserts the girl he's almost engaged to, cuckolds his best friend, and generally mismanages his life, feeling himself all the while somehow redeemed by his attraction to a married woman he doesn't have the will power even to seduce. What does Flaubert hope to gain by offering such a guide to a Paris torn by a dozen different wild political theories?

Henry James, in *Notes on Novelists,* took Flaubert to task for picking such flawed characters as Emma and Frédéric Moreau as the principal subjects of his fiction.

> Our complaint is that Emma Bovary, in spite of the nature of her consciousness and in spite of her reflecting so much that of her creator, is really too small an affair. This, critically speaking, is in view both of the value and fortune of her history, a wonderful circumstance. She associates herself with Frédéric Moreau in *L'Éducation* to suggest for us a question that can be answered, I hold, only to Flaubert's detriment. Emma taken alone would possibly not so directly press it, but in her company the hero of our author's second study of the "real" drives it home. Why did Flaubert choose, as special conduits of the life he proposed to depict, such inferior, and in the case of Frédéric such abject human specimen?

I cannot agree with James about Emma, but I certainly do about Frédéric. What is the difference? I suggest that it lies essentially in the fact that Emma is a woman. And to some extent, at least, her doom has been determined by the conditions of her early life. She is a motherless only child, educated in a convent by ignorant and bigoted nuns and allowed to wallow in mushy romantic fiction. She emerges from the convent to find herself isolated on her father's farm, where she meets no eligible suitor but a dull and stupid doctor. Once married to him, she sees the rest of her life unfolding in the deadly ennui of a small gossiping village. Granted that she does everything possible to make a dim future dimmer, she still has some of the pathos of a wild bird in a cage.

Frédéric Moreau, on the other hand, starts life with a deck of trump cards. He has good looks, intelligence, an indulgent parent, and a fortune with which to enjoy in idleness the delights of Parisian life. And what does he do with every bright chance that comes his way but make utter hash of it? All one wants to give Frédéric at the end of his tale is what Henry James wanted to give the typical hero of a Paul Bourget novel: *un coup de pied dans le derrière*.

If one murmurs "how terrible" over the fate of Emma, one only shrugs over that of Frédéric. To me he adds force to the argument that a character can be too inane to support a great novel. Edward A. Robinson would have handled him in a short poem as he did his immortal Miniver Cheevy.

Anthony Trollope

NTHONY TROLLOPE'S HEARTY and embracing personality pervades his fiction as densely as Dickens's does his. His reader is never left without the assurance, endlessly emphasized, that English squires, English maidens, English sports, and English traditions are the finest in the world. There is nothing, he reiterates, quite as high-minded or as honorable as a true English gentleman of proper breeding and ancient lineage. Yet Trollope is never bullheadedly insular or blind to national faults. In *The Way We Live Now* he lambastes the current obsession in the City in London with money and profit; in the Barchester novels he excoriates the worldliness of the clergy as evidenced by Vesey Stanhope and Obadiah Slope, and, for all his respect for the peerage and the divisions of a class society, there are no two more odious noblemen in fiction than Earl DeCourcy in *The Small House at Allington* or the Marquis of Brotherton in *Is He Popenjoy?* And it is also true that Trollope's post office work took him on global tours to the West Indies, Egypt, South Africa, Australia, New Zealand, and the United States and gave him material for his travel books.

It might be pointed out, however, that in *The Way We Live Now,* the novel in which Trollope most fiercely attacks aspects of British life, in which he savagely indicts the commercial profligacy that he fears has undermined business enterprise, he places the prime responsibility on a foreigner, Augustus Melmotte, a monster of duplicity and presumably a Jew. One cannot quite escape the suggestion that the British, left to themselves, might not have fallen quite so low.

Trollope's prototype of the best that England could provide was the squire whose substantial farm had been in his family for generations and who was proudly content to manage it efficiently and to take a benevolent interest in the affairs of the surrounding and sometimes dependent local community. He hunted and dined with the neighboring gentry and nobility, respecting but in no way kowtowing to peers and bishops, and he would have lost a fortune rather than break his word. It goes without saying that he feared nobody and nothing, and that he despised fops, flatterers, snobs, and social climbers and didn't hesitate to show it. A reader may be willing to sympathize with Trollope's values, and even to like him for them, but there are times when he may feel that they may be being trumpeted at the expense of others.

I offer in illustration of my thesis two of his finest novels: *The Small House at Allington* and *The Duke's Children.* In the former his "good" characters are very good indeed. Squire Dale may be a bit grumpy and overly sensitive, but he is as true blue as other Trollopian squires; his sister-in-law Mary and her two daughters, Belle and Lily, are beautiful, virtuous, and brave, and Johnny Eames, the hero, though something of a hobbledehoy before he matures, and inclined, as Trollope tolerantly puts it, to do those things which young men should not do, is in all other respects a thoroughly likeable, spirited, and courageous youth who can save an old man from a raging bull and give the villain a black eye. Trollope seems almost cozily to identify himself with him. When Johnny is obliged by his employers to take his holiday in October, his creator observes: "For myself, I always regard May as the best month for holiday-making, but then no Londoner cares to be absent in May."

It is, however, by means of a flawed character that Trollope brings out all that is most interesting in his good ones and effectively saves his novel from the pitfalls of sentimentality. Adolphus Crosbie is the victim of his own weak character: he knows not only what is morally right but also what will contribute most to his own happiness: carrying out his engagement to the lovely but penniless and socially obscure Lily Dale, who adores him and whom he loves as much as such a man as he can love. Yet he cannot lure himself from the lure of rank: Lady Alexandrina DeCourcy, as he perfectly sees, is possessed of a mean and selfish character and offers only a trifling dowry, but she is an earl's daughter. And for this he will incur disgrace and unpopularity and find himself wed to a discontented woman who will leave him in a matter of weeks! Trollope brilliantly understands the plight of a villain who hasn't the force and malice to be a successful villain. "It was in this that Crosbie's failure had been so grievous—that he had seen and approved the better course, but had chosen for himself to walk in that which was worse."

Trollope sadly disappointed many of his devoted fans by not giving Lily Dale to her true lover, Johnny Eames, in the end, but he chose to represent her—even admiringly—as faithful for life to her love for the rotter who had jilted her. There may have been a place for this in Victorian mores, but to us today she seems to have made a pointless and foolish sacrifice. *The Small House* is still, however, one of Trollope's best.

The Duke's Children has much in it that is hard for a modern reader, particularly a modern American reader, to swallow. The Duke of Omnium is represented as a nobleman of the utmost probity and public spirit, a former prime minister who has served his nation more out of duty than ambition, yet who is shy, reserved, dry and cold of manner, uninterested in sports (rare for a sympathetic Trollope character), and very conscious of his exalted rank and vast fortune as things requiring his children to mate in the same milieu. This last he carries to the point of refusing to sanction the marriage of his daughter to a splendid young man of good but not noble rank and small means, and that of his elder son and heir to a beautiful, talented, and virtuous American heiress whose father is spoken of as a potential presidential candidate. And this is the man whom Trollope makes no bones of admiring above all the other characters of his extensive fiction! One's Yankee blood begins to stir a bit.

Of course, the Duke has to give in at last and to sanction both alliances, but he does so with a minimum of grace, saying to his heir, a' propos of the latter's younger brother: "I suppose Gerald will now bring me a kitchen maid." Yet Trollope makes it clear that the lovely American heiress, in his opinion, is getting a prize. But what is she really getting? The Duke's heir, Lord Silverbridge, is handsome enough, yes, even gloriously handsome if that's all she wants, but he is also blunt, naive, unimaginative, addicted to sports and gambling (he has already lost a fortune in horse races), a trivial amateur in politics, and he is half-engaged to another girl when he proposes to the American. Yet to Trollope his looks and birth seem to make up for everything else. And the American girl will one day be Duchess of Omnium! To some it looks like elementary snobbishness.

The American Senator contains similar problems for Trollope's audience on this side of the Atlantic. It may be safer to read him in the far greater body of his wonderful fiction where his passionate loyalty to the England of empire dominance has less to quicken a republican pulse.

Nathaniel Hawthorne

A GREAT DEAL HAS BEEN WRITTEN about the mystery of Nathaniel Hawthorne's personality, and some critics have even gone so far as to surmise that there may have been a secret side of his nature that he was guarding from his friends and family. If there be any answer to such speculations it might well be sought in his masterpiece, the hauntingly beautiful and seamlessly constructed *Scarlet Letter.* For certainly that tale is open to different interpretations.

We can start by analyzing the exact nature of the heroine's offense to the moral and legal code of the Massachusetts Bay Colony in the 1640s. Hester Prynne was a virtuous and noble-minded young English woman living in Amsterdam and married childlessly to an elderly and partially crippled scholar whom she venerated but did not love. Her marriage had been one of convenience, and she had accepted it. When her husband decided to immigrate to the New World, he sent her on ahead, while he remained for a time "to look after some necessary affairs," but promising soon to follow. He did not follow, however, and it seemed likely that he had been lost at sea—a common enough fate for those who ventured to cross the Atlantic—and Hester found herself in the anomalous position of being a beautiful single woman with a possibly still living husband in a small Puritan Boston. After the passage of a year or more she fell in love with a handsome and deeply spiritual bachelor minister, Arthur Dimmesdale, the idol of the community, who returned her passion, and the two embarked on a clandestine love affair which resulted in her pregnancy. Hester insisted that he should remain anonymous in the affair, allowing her to bear the disgrace alone, on the theory that he must not destroy his value to the adoring members of his flock. Reluctantly, his conscience torn, he agreed to her plan.

As Hester was known to be the wife of a man not proven dead, the crime exposed by her condition was not merely fornication but adultery for which in Puritan Boston the penalty was capital, as can be seen by modern readers of Governor John Winthrop's diary in an entry describing the arraignment and hanging of a couple so accused. But because of the ameliorating circumstance of her husband's disappearance, Hester is sentenced only to the public disgrace of wearing the token of her sin on her breast for life and standing with her baby for some hours on the town scaffold exposed to the scornful gaze of the crowd.

All of this, of course, does not strike a modern reader as a crime at all. And even in 1850, when the novel was published, it was hardly an unforgivable one. But of course Hawthorne, as an historical novelist, was correct in setting forth the horror and contempt with which Bostonians of the 1640s regarded it. What may surprise a reader today is how clearly, however much he may deprecate the rigor of Hester's punishment and the cruelty and occasional hypocrisy of her tormentors, he seems to share their view of the gravity of her guilt.

He concedes, it is true, that her judges are harsh. "Out of the whole human family, it would not have been easy to select the same number of wise and virtuous persons who should be less capable of sitting in judgment on an erring woman's heart and disentangling its mesh of good and evil than the sages of rigid aspect towards whom Hester now turned her face." But he is quick to emphasize the moral contrast between the "image of Divine Maternity" so finely represented by the greatest painters, and the sorry picture of Hester standing before the sneering crowd, her bastard child in her arms. "Here was the taint of deepest sin in the most sacred quality of human life, working such effect that the world was only the darker for this woman's beauty, and the more lost for the infant she had borne."

What Hester thought of her supposed guilt we shall come to, but there is no doubt that her lover shared the feelings of the crowd. Calling upon her to reveal his part in the affair, he actually envies her for her suffering: "Heaven hath granted thee an open ignominy, that thereby thou mayest work out an open triumph over the evil within thee, and the sorrow without." He has no doubt that they have committed a mortal sin.

Hester has a different view. There is in her nature "a rich, voluptuous, Oriental characteristic—a taste for the gorgeously beautiful" which her creator is far from finding exempt from fault, perhaps fearing the lion's share of it in his own personality. In Hester it finds expression in her needlework. Hawthorne goes on to say: "Women derive a pleasure, incomprehensible to the other sex, from the delicate toil of the needle. To Hester Prynne it might have been a mode of expressing, and therefore soothing, the passion of her life. Like all other joys she rejected it as a sin. "This morbid meddling of conscience with an immaterial matter betokened, it is to be feared, no genuine and steadfast penitence, but something doubtful, something that might be deeply wrong beneath." To be feared by whom? By Hawthorne himself.

He even suggests that Hester's disillusionment as to virtue in other women was attributable to her own downfall. "O Fiend, whose talisman was that fatal symbol, wouldst thou leave nothing, whether in youth or age, for this poor sinner to revere?—such loss of faith is ever one of the saddest results of sin." Hawthorne supposes that adultery has bound her to support her lover in his trials. "Here was the iron link of mutual crime, which neither he nor she could break. Like all other ties, it brought along with it its obligations."

There is no question that Hawthorne expects us to admire Hester's indomitable courage and resolution in facing her isolation from the community and her selfless generosity in returning good for bad, as witnessed by her tending and nursing even those poor and sick souls who despise the hand that succors them. But when the heroine's life begins to turn from passion and feeling to thought, when she discovers that the world's law has no law for the mind, when she dares in her speculations to undermine the very foundations of the Puritan establishment and to discern that the whole system of society must be torn up and built anew for women to take their proper place in it, Hawthorne fears that she has lost the way to true penitence, that she "was wandering without a clue in the dark labyrinth of mind" and was even wondering if she should not put an end to her and her child's existence. "The scarlet letter," he concludes grimly, "had not done its office."

It is clear then that Hawthorne gravely faults Hester for her failure properly to rue her deed. He asks the reader: "Had seven long years, under the torture of the scarlet letter, inflicted so much of misery and wrought out no repentance?" And when Hester goes to meet Dimmesdale in the forest and casts the token of her disgrace to the withered leaves, Hawthorne fears that she is compounding her sin. "It may be that it was the talisman of a stern and severe, but yet a guardian spirit, who now forsook her, as recognizing that, in spite of his strict watch over her heart, some new evil had crept into it, or some old one had never been expelled." Hester even tries to justify their act to her lover when she exclaims: "What we did had a consecration of its own." And she plans to flee the colony with him.

But this is only a renewal of their adultery, and it is frustrated—fortunately, no doubt, in the author's point of view—by Dimmesdale's public confession and death. In the end Hawthorne sums up the case against Hester:

> She had wandered, without rule or guidance, in a moral wilderness, as vast, as intricate and as shadowy, as the untamed forest. . . . Her intellect and heart had their home, as it were, in desert places, where she roamed as freely as the wild Indian in his woods. For years past she had looked from the estranged point of view at human institutions, and whatever priests or legislators had established, criticizing with hardly more reverence than the Indian would feel for the clerical band, the judicial robe, the pillory, the gallows, the fireside, or the church. The tendency of her fate and fortunes had been to set her free. The scarlet letter was her passport into regions where other woman dared not tread. Shame, despair, solitude! These had been her teachers—stern and wild ones—and they had made her strong, but taught her much amiss.

But that is not the final judgment that I derive from the novel. It leaves me with the picture of a brave and passionate woman gloriously liberated by cruel suffering from the bondage of ignorance and superstition and taking her place in the freer intellectual atmosphere that was dawning in the Europe she had left behind. The dark forest that surrounds and threatens to engulf the small, struggling New England colony represents the wild force of uninhibited nature, and the Puritan community symbolizes the desperate effort of man to impose some kind of order upon it. Hester's flight to the woods is her attempted escape from the rigors of the arbitrary moral code of the pioneers. But it is doomed, and Hawthorne appears to take his stand with the elders of the colony.

But does he really? This to me is the question that pervades his book and gives it much of its peculiar flavor and interest. Hawthorne's personality was a deeply divided one. On the one hand, as a romantic and a lover of colorful history, he greatly admired the rugged Puritans, true to their stern God and resolute faith, bravely fortifying their little settlement against the dark menace of the surrounding wilderness and also against the intrusion of modern heresies from the Old World on which they had turned their backs. He found a greater appeal in the Massachusetts Bay Colony than he did in what he regarded as the shallower, more material, and often irreverent society of contemporary Boston. His loyalty was essentially to the past, and his religion was the old one.

But there was the other Hawthorne, the intellectual curious scholar who was deeply interested in, if not always approving of, the tumultuous changes of his own day, and the author of a campaign biography of his close friend President Franklin Pierce. This side of Hawthorne is in constant and obvious sympathy with his heroine in every step of her story. How he reconciled in his own mind and heart such sympathy with the sternness of his inherited and cherished puritanical moral code must have been through his unpuritanical belief in a divine mercy that would redeem both Hester and her persecutors. It may have been this same faith that made him refer the question of slavery to the Almighty in his much—and to my mind justly—criticized answer to the abolitionists in his life of Pierce in 1852:

> But there is still another view, and probably as wise a one. It looks upon slavery as one of those evils which divine Providence does not leave to be remedied by human contrivances, but which, in its own good time, by some means impossible to be anticipated, but of the simplest and easiest operation, when all its uses have been fulfilled, it causes to vanish like a dream.

Theodore Dreiser

WHEN HENRY JAMES revisited his native land in 1905, after an absence of twenty years, he did not much relish the social and architectural changes that he described in *The American Scene*. But what he importantly saw in the new century was that it was essentially a people's time. Make no mistake, he warned his readers, the "people" liked the noise, the racket, the crowding, the rush, the push, the availability of new gadgets, the sentimentality of public entertainment, the promiscuity of human contact. For all its tycoons and robber barons, America was still at heart a people's republic. And James at the end had no desire to be a part of it. When he went home to the blessed solitude and quiet of his beloved Lamb House in Rye on the English Channel, it was to be for good.

Theodore Dreiser wrote of the same era that James described, but he saw it not through the eyes of an elderly and Europeanized expatriate, but through those of an embittered and originally underprivileged native. He fully recognized the qualities in America that James detested: the crassness, the commercialization, the standardization of everything, the rampant vulgarity, but he understood in his heart why it all appealed to people who had started like with little or nothing. Dreiser is one of the few American writers who makes his reader actually feel the appeal to the have-not of the meretricious glitter of the tacky store window, the tarnished splendor of a middling hotel lobby, the gilded pomposity of the popular men's bar. Sinclair Lewis describes such things with all the hate and contempt that he felt for them; Dreiser, in his youth anyway, had succumbed to their lure. He is a kind of American Zola.

Here is how he sees Sister Carrie, the heroine of her eponymous novel, on her first arrival in Chicago, wandering enviously through a department store:

Carrie passed along the busy aisles, much affected by the remarkable display of trinkets, dress goods, stationery and jewelry. Each separate counter was a show place of dazzling interest and attraction. She could not help feeling the claim of each trinket and valuable upon her personality, and yet she did not stop. There was nothing there which she could not have used—nothing which she did not long to own. The dainty slippers and stockings, the delicately frilled skirts and petticoats, the laces, ribbons, hair-combs, purses, all touched her with personal desire, and she felt keenly the fact that not any of these things were in the range of her purchase. . . . She realized in a dim way how much the city held—wealth, fashion, ease—every adornment for women, and she longed for dress and beauty with a whole heart.

And here is Dreiser's own reflection on the "gorgeous saloon" of which Carrie's soon-to-be seducer, Hurstwood, is the magnificent proprietor:

Yet, here is the fact of the lighted chamber, the dressy, greedy company, the small, self-interested palaver, the disorganized, aimless, wandering mental action which it represents—the love of light and show and finery which, to one outside, under the serene light of the eternal stars, must seem a strange and shiny thing. Under the stars and sweeping night winds, what a lamp-flower it must bloom; a strange, glittering night-flower, odour-yielding, insect-drawing, insect-infected rose of pleasure.

Clyde Griffiths in *An American Tragedy* sees in his first glimpse of the interior of an opulent hotel a heaven not yet available to him:

There, at midnight even, before each of the three principal entrances—one facing each of the three streets—was a doorman in a long maroon coat with many buttons and a high-rimmed and long-visored maroon cap. And inside, behind looped and fluted French silk curtains, were the still blazing lights, the à la carte dining room and the American grill near one corner still open. And about them were many taxis and cars. And there was music always—from somewhere.

As Clyde rises socially through his connection with a rich uncle in Lycurgus, New York, he finds himself on the threshold of a life in a rich lakeside resort that was beyond his wildest dreams as a boy. Will he see through it to its vanity and vacuity? Never. There is no disillusionment for one so starved for the decorations of life. Heaven is at last attainable, and murder is not too great a price for him to pay for it.

Pavilions by the shore. An occasional slender pier reaching out for some spacious and at times stately summer lodge, such as those now owned by the Cranstons, Finchleys and others. The green and blue canoes and launches. The gay hotel and pavilion at Pine Point already smartly attended by the early arrivals here! And then the pier and boathouse of the Cranston Lodge itself, with two Russian wolfhounds recently acquired by Bertine lying on the grass near the shore, apparently waiting for her return, and a servant, John, one of a half dozen who attended the family here, waiting to take the single bag of Clyde, his tennis racquet and golf sticks. But most of all he was impressed by the large rambling and yet smartly designed house, with its bright, geranium-bordered walks, its wide, brown, wicker-studded veranda commanding a beautiful view of the lake, the cars and personalities of the various guests, who in golf, tennis or lounging clothes were to be seen idling here and there.

Dreiser is something of a determinist. His characters live in the world as he, through a straightened and difficult youth, had come to see it. To a large extent their destinies are shaped by the conditions in which they were born. Sister Carrie can only escape from a dreary life in the tiny stifling apartment of her tedious sister and brother-in-law, chained to a soul-destroying, twelve-hour-a day job in a shoe factory, by becoming the mistress of two comparatively rich men. Ultimately she will attain the independence of a successful stage career, but not until the second of her lovers has been brought to ruin by abandoning his wife and career for her. Carrie is a passive, kindly creature with no desire to hurt anyone; she simply allows herself to be borne along in the current that appears to be rescuing her from a life of misery.

Her moral sense is certainly tepid. Dreiser, at least at this point of his life, seems to have seen the moral imperative as a problem, if it is one at all, only for the managerial sections of human society. The great sweating majority had little use for it if it ever came between them and the chance to improve their dismal lot. Dreiser does not blame them for this. One has no particular sense that he thinks that Carrie is doing anything very wrong in leaving one man for another, or even that Hurstwood is, when he steals from his employers to finance his near abduction of Carrie. He will be caught and punished; that will be enough for him. He has stumbled into a crime for which he was neither trained nor prepared, and he has bungled it disastrously. Both the bungling and the crime were parts of the fate that was determined by what, when, and where he was born. Dreiser, the determinist, has pity for the victims of fate, but he is well aware that pity isn't going to do them much good.

Clyde Griffiths has much more moral sense than Carrie, but then he has been raised by parents who passionately believed in the validity of their shabby Christian Mission House and in the efficacy of their humble and futile street preaching to faintly curious itinerants. Clyde has only scorn for a faith he doesn't share and a proselytizing that humiliates him, but he never questions the sincerity of his progenitors. He simply wants to break away and soon does. But when he evolves the desperate plan to drown his pregnant mistress to be free to wed the heiress who is enamored of him, he would be a monster indeed if he felt no compunction. Of course, he feels it, and it even causes him to change his mind at the last moment, though not in time to save his victim from a semi-accidental death.

Dreiser does not in the least excuse Clyde; he leaves him, as he leaves Hurstwood, to the terrible consequences of his incompetently executed crime. The crime and its bungled handling are both, it would seem, integral parts of a life preordained by the circumstances of the actor's origin. Dreiser simply stands back and tells us that this is what America gives rise to. He indeed feels for the unfortunate, be they criminals or the victims of criminals, but that is the way things are.

He has only kind words for Clyde's afflicted mother, and he has a tolerance, somewhat tempered by condescension, for her deep Christian faith, but as an agnostic, if not an atheist, at this time in his life, he could not imagine that religion could do much more than ease an occasional ache.

If we turn now to Dreiser's novels about Frank Cowperwood, the streetcar magnate, *The Financier* and *The Titan,* we see a different aspect of Dreiser's personality: his candid admiration of the man who takes hold of his own destiny and tears it from the grip of the determinist. Cowperwood is cool, calculating, and ruthless when the occasion calls for ruthlessness. He seizes the businesses he wants and the women he wants, but he is always honest with himself, devoid of self-pity, and as fair in his financial dealings as a successful tycoon can be in an era of unbridled laisser-faire. Like the African wild dog, he kills only what he needs to eat, and he kills quickly. And he is always devastatingly attractive. In short, he is a noble and magnificent animal. Dreiser, the determinist, in these novels has shown himself an existentialist.

He may have come to see that the development of the country should not be left, or certainly not solely left, to robber barons like Cowperwood. It may have had to do with the author's later dallying with communism. But whatever his leftist leanings they did not produce great novels.

Jean Racine

I T IS HARD TO IMAGINE an art form less adapted to the disclosure of a writer's personality than the French classic tragedy. The time of the action is limited to twenty-four hours, the setting to a single site, the language to a few hundred permissible words, and the characters must confine themselves to speaking—they may not *do* anything. Yet Jean Racine was always perfectly comfortable within these restrictions; the beauty of his verse seemed actually enhanced by them, as roses may be by a skillfully designed formal garden. It may have been his very ease with the form that kept it going so many years after his death, even in the hands of playwrights who had manifest difficulty with it.

Yet Racine, in his two most famous female protagonists, Phèdre and Athalie, managed, perhaps unconsciously, to reveal a dynamic aspect of his own personality. It will be remembered that his emotional life fell roughly into two periods: the more or less flaming early years of his dramatic successes and his affair with a famous actress, and the sober later ones where he was converted to a stricter Catholicism and induced to abandon the theatre except for two dramas taken from biblical sources. These latter years witnessed his marriage to a middle-class matron of the utmost respectability and his employment by the king as an historiographer. *Phèdre* belongs to the first era—indeed it marks the end of it—and *Athalie* to the second. But in both plays I seem to feel the poet's enduring sympathy with all that he had most rigorously repressed in his own personality. God might have willed the drastic change in his life—God and Madame de Maintenon—but there were still things that he was always going to miss.

The appalling thing to me about Racine's recovered faith: a Catholicism tainted with Jansenism and even a dose of Calvinism—though the latter he would have vigorously repudiated—is that to him the souls that were saved were not necessarily the most virtuous, nor were those that were damned necessarily the most wicked. The divine judgment, it must have seemed to him, could be arbitrary at will. For he certainly goes out of his way to exculpate Phèdre as the helpless victim of Venus, the implacable goddess who has entrapped her in sin. Yet Phèdre is nonetheless presumably damned.

Consider her case. Stricken with a sudden and overpowering lust for her beautiful stepson, Hippolyte, she does everything in her power to repress her passion. She builds a proprietary temple to the goddess, orders hecatombs of sacrifices in her name, refuses to have any relations with Hippolyte, even forbidding his name to be mentioned in her presence, and finally, by shrill appeals to her husband, succeeds in banishing him from the court. It all avails her nothing. Her eyes continue to find his likeness in the features of his father, and Thésée, repenting of his harshness to a beloved son, revokes his exile. Phèdre, exhausted now by her struggle with herself, weakened by sleeplessness and fast, hopes only to die, and seems on the verge of extinction.

And then what happens? Thésée goes off on one of his amorous expeditions—a further excuse for Phèdre is his constant infidelity—and fails to return. The rumor of his death is generally taken for a certainty. Phèdre's old nurse and confidant Oenone urges her to pull herself together in the interests of her young son, now king of Athens. She points out that her husband's demise has removed the guilt of her love for his son: "Votre flamme devient une flamme ordinaire." Phèdre must meet with Hippolyte to discuss the problems of the heritage.

Of course, in the discussion that ensues Phèdre breaks down and blurts out her love to the appalled young man in a torrent of burning phrases. He promptly quits her presence, leaving her rejected, disgraced, and trembling with indignation at the scorn and contempt that she has read in his flashing eyes.

On top of this deadly blow comes the news that Thésée is alive, after all, and about to reappear in the palace. What to do? Oenone hastily advises her that the best defense is attack: she must forestall the danger of Hippolyte's denunciation of herself by accusing him of attempted rape. Thésée can be counted on not to be too hard on the young man: "Un père en punissant est toujours père." Phèdre, half dead with confusion and shame, weakly agrees.

Now this, of course, to a modern reader, is Phèdre's real crime, and indeed her only one. Yet surely it is to some extent ameliorated by the danger and humiliation of her situation, by the blow to her pride incurred by her stepson's disgusted rejection of her advances, by Oenone's reassuring argument, and by the shattered state of her own health. And almost immediately afterwards, fearing—and with justification—that Thésée may actually seek his son's death —she hurries to her husband to plead for him, ready, if necessary to confess that she has lied, only to have Hippolyte's love for Aricie, hitherto unknown to her, flung in her face. In her wild fury she contemplates asking Thésée to renew his old revenge on Aricie and her politically adverse family, but stops, recognizing at last how far her passion has carried her. And now she utters the final threnody of her despair.

> Mes crimes désormais ont comblé la mesure.
> Je respire à la fois l'inceste et l'imposture.
> Mes homicides mains, promptes à me venger,
> Dans le sang innocent brûlent de se plonger.
> Miserable! et je vis? et je soutiens la vue
> De ce sacré soleil dont je suis descendue?
> J'ai pour aieul le père et le maître des dieux:
> Le ciel, tout l'univers est plein de mes aieux.
> Où me cacher? Fuyons dans la nuit infernale.
> Mais que dis-je? Mon père y tient l'urne fatale.

She rightly observes that a cruel god has doomed her family. And that god's final blow is this: that she has never enjoyed the fruit of her deadly crime.

Neptune delivers the unfortunate Hippolyte to his death, acquitting himself of an old obligation to Thésée, and Phèdre, having taken a fatal poison, expires in the presence of her husband after a full confession.

> Et la mort, à mes yeux, dérobant la clarté,
> Rend aux jours qu'ils souillaient toute sa pureté.

The exquisite peacefulness of Phèdre's last lines indicates to me Racine's inner acceptance of the anguish of a soul born to bear and die for a sin thrust upon it by a deity, Venus, who must be reverenced and adored even if she be never accountable for her acts. Yet these lines give me no sense of an impending hell. They seem rather to predict a void, a nothingness, or perhaps what Walter Pater described in "Sebastian Van Storck" as "the warm presence of life, the cry of humanity itself" being "no more than a troubling irritation of the surface of the one absolute mind," the latter being likened to a "pallid arctic sun disclosing itself over the dead level of a glacial, a barren, an absolutely lonely sea."

Queen Athalie of Joam in her tragedy is, of course, a far more wicked soul than Phèdre, but even her crimes were committed under circumstances that call for some amelioration. In her war with the Jews she had seen her father and brother slaughtered, her mother thrown to the dogs from a high window, and her allies massacred, and she had retaliated by killing her own children and grandchildren because they were descended from the hated Jewish King David. The Jews were fighting for Jehovah; she for Baal; there was no mercy on either side. But she had succeeded in bringing prosperity to her people, and now she was intent on bringing peace to her dominions, offering to the Jews under her rule the same tolerance that she expected—vainly—from them. She had been indeed a bloody, ruthless and formidable despot, but that was the way of her world, as the books of the Old Testament make only too clear.

Athalie shows herself almost pitifully tortured by a terrible dream of her mother's grisly end and her own approaching one, and she is genuinely touched by the boy Joas whom she is anxious to bring up as her own heir in order to secure peace. She shows herself at her best when she asks the lad if he has no boyish pleasure and if his god requires uninterrupted worship and reverence. She assures him that he will be free to worship as he chooses in her palace, but she reserves the same right for herself. Together, she tells him, they will have two powerful gods. But in the end, of course, she is trapped and slaughtered. She can hardly expect to prevail over Jehovah; Racine, the Bible, and the high priest Joad have guaranteed that Baal is only a brass idol.

But Athalie, unlike Phèdre, is defiant, and magnificently so, crying: "Dieu, des Juifs, tu l'emportes!" She recognizes that she is no match for a Jewish deity who can use a child to pluck her heart strings for her own undoing, but she dies with a terrible curse on her lips, foretelling that Joas will grow up to be a tyrant worse than all the others—which, of course, occurs.

Racine conformed to a Catholic god and to a pious Madame de Maintenon; he accepted the salvations and damnations of the contemporary church. But in his art he reserved a space for his respect, perhaps his nostalgia, for the passions and drama of his youth.

Henry James

ENRY JAMES, perhaps more than any other writer, was concerned with seeing life through fiction. It has often been observed that he and Edith Wharton emanated from the same social background because they spent much of their early days in New York and Newport, though twenty years apart. But Wharton's milieu was one of wealth and old brownstone respectability, whereas that of the James family was totally intellectual and unworldly. Henry James, Senior, had inherited enough money to be free of toil, and he took full advantage of this situation to liberate his children, not only from business, which all of his many siblings and their offspring equally disdained, but also from any social prejudices which might interfere with the free play of a bold and inquiring mind. The elder James was a close friend of Emerson and Carlyle; discussions at the family board were lively and stimulating. The young Henry was encouraged to read everything he wanted, and he devoured contemporary novels, living for the next serial of Thackeray or Dickens or the next issue of the *Revue des Deux Mondes*.

Of course, having eyes and ears that missed nothing, Henry had an early sense that his family were not like other people. His father, for example, had no occupation that would be readily understood by the boys at the various New York City schools that he attended. When he asked his father what he could tell them his father did, the latter's replies were not helpful. "Say I'm a philosopher, say I'm a seeker for truth, say I'm a lover of any kind, say I'm an author of books if you like; or, best of all, just say I'm a student." Similarly, in a world where everybody belonged to a church of some denomination and regularly attended Sunday service, the Jameses, though cultivating an atmosphere of faith, belonged to no temple of worship. As Henry was later to put it: "I was troubled all along by this particular crookedness of our being so extremely religious without having, as it were, anything in the least classified or striking to show for it, so that the measure of other-worldliness pervading our premises was rather a waste." Yet Henry seems not to have suffered anything more than a mild embarrassment at his family's standing so apart from the crowd.

There are several possible reasons for this. His family, together with the vast cousinage, many of whom shared the senior Henry's eccentricities, formed a solid and loyal phalanx to back up any member who might suffer the least social ostracism. Second was the fact that Henry was never sent to a boarding school; there was always a definite limit to the punishment that day school boys could inflict on a nonconformist, and every afternoon he was reunited with his loving family. And then there were the long stays in England, France, and Switzerland where an array of foreign tutors and briefly attended foreign academies may have had the effect of making it appear to the boy that the only real world, at least insofar as he was concerned, was that of his parents and siblings, and that the rest was simply a fascinating passing pageant that it would be his joy and his genius one day to portray. Henry believed that his essential role in life as an observer had been predicted by his having seen and remembered, as a child under two, from a carriage window in Paris, a tall column in a square, which he later identified as the elevated statue of Napoleon in the Place Vendôme.

His father, really, was too broadminded. He was even reluctant to have his sons adopt a profession, fearing that any such might diminish the openness of the mind to new thought and experience. Henry, except for a brief dalliance with painting in Newport, wisely discouraged by his older friend and mentor, John Lafarge, who saw his true bent, was politely deferential to what his mother always called "your father's ideas," despite his exclusive absorption in reading and writing fiction. He passively in Geneva bowed to the paternal suggestion that he study engineering, just as later he spent a year in Harvard Law School, but in each case it was at most lip service that he offered the new discipline, keeping the bulk of his time and all of his energy for his true muse.

That literature might prove a lonely realm, that it might lead one to eschew the thrills and dangers of action, did not make it less attractive to him. Years later he was to write to Moreton Fullerton: "The port from which I set out, was, I think, that of the *essential loneliness of my life,* and it seems to be the port, also, in sooth to which my course again finally directs itself! This loneliness (since I mention it!)—what is it still but the deepest thing about one? Deeper about me, at any rate, than anything else: deeper than my 'genius,' deeper than

my 'discipline,' deeper than my pride, deeper, above all, than the deep coun-
termining of art."

And it was on the ears of this grave eighteen-year-old, living, as I have said,
for the next issue of the *Revue des Deux Mondes,* that the news of the firing
on Fort Sumter on April 12. 1861 fell. In *Notes of a Son and Brother,* written
more than forty years later, James describes the "confusion established in my
consciousness during the soft spring of '61 by the firing on Fort Sumter, Mr.
Lincoln's instant first call for volunteers and a physical mishap, already referred
to as having overtaken me at the same dark hour, and the effects of which
were to draw themselves out incalculably and intolerably." The mishap, presumably to James's back, occurred when he was pumping an antiquated fire
engine to help put out a fire in Newport.

But the fire, well documented, happened six months after Sumter, and there
is no evidence that the able-bodied, sturdily hiking young James made any
move to answer Lincoln's call in the interim. To the older man, writing his
memoirs, it seemed clear that the injury, whatever it was, that would keep
him from combat was an integral part and parcel of the war, that his pain was
a portion of the general pain, and that he had participated in the conflict in
a sense no less real for being imagined. The accident had in "twenty odious
minutes" made of what might have seemed "disparities," that is, what was
happening to James and what was happening to the nation, "a single vast
visitation."

He saw, however, how others might view his condition. How could any
young man, apparently healthy to the uninformed observer, not fight? And
had not an eminent surgeon in Boston pooh-poohed his complaint when his
father had taken him to Boston for a diagnosis? With youth around him leap-
ing to the colors, "to have trumped up a lameness at such a juncture could
be made to pass in no way for graceful." James remained at home, with occasional trips to Boston and New York for the next two years. It was not until
July of 1863 that his name came before the Selective Service Board, and then
he was exempted on grounds of health.

We know that back pains are subject to remissions and that a man who
can move freely at times might well be rejected by the military if his liabil-
ity to crippling attacks disqualified him for long marches. But when one
remembers the desperate ruses that some men with physical flaws invented
to fool the draft boards in World War II into passing over them for military
service, one harbors the suspicion that James may have rather complacently
accepted his deferment. He led an apparently normal life, and shortly after

Appomattox we read of his taking long hikes again. I am fairly sure that he believed that he was unfit for combat, but I also suspect that he was secretly glad to be so and happy to be reserved for the wonderful life of letters that was just beginning to seem a possibility to him. And we should be happy that he was. He would have been a rotten soldier, and it is ghastly to think of him lying as a corpse on the red dirt of Virginia with all those books unwritten.

What is less charming, however, at least to me, is James's desire to convince himself and us that he *did* play a kind of role in the war. In 1862 he enrolled in Harvard Law School, and the similarity of a crowd of students to a host of troops seems to have assuaged his sense of alienation. "I well recall, for that matter, how when early in the autumn I had in fact become the queerest of forensic recruits, the bristling hordes of my Law School comrades fairly produced the illusion of a mustered army." But what he really liked was the illusion of a mustered army of noncombatants, even of shirkers, to cover his own immunity, for he adds, "how easily it let me down that when it came to the point one had still fine, fierce young men, in great numbers, for company, there being at the worst so many such who hadn't flown to arms."

One wishes at this point that he would be silent. It is hard not to be reminded of his two younger brothers who fought and whose lives were permanently crippled by the experience. James shouldn't ask for the same sympathy we afford the wounded. But he is remorseless. He wants the same stars as if he were a veteran. One of his only contacts with the war was a single day's visit to an army hospital in Portsmouth Grove in Rhode Island, where he sat by the beds of some wounded and distributed a bit of cash. On the boat returning to Newport he suffered pain from his exertion and felt that it crowned his "little adventure of sympathy," as it brought him the consoling realization that, measuring wounds for wounds, "one was no less exaltedly than wastefully engaged in the common fact of endurance." This is greedy. He wanted to have his cake of military exemption and to eat it too.

Yet wasn't this attitude also an inherent part of James the artist? The need to upgrade, to dignify, the role of the observer, to give it equal value to that of the participant? James reached out to seize all that was emotionally beautiful in the agony and sacrifice of war, wrapping himself in the banners of conflict and making it, to the extent of which his magnificent imagination was capable, *his* war. But there was in it a touch of the false, like the comment of the bereaved British mother in Noel Coward's *Cavalcade* that the uplifting shared emotion of the home front in World War I had "made strange heaven out of unbelievable hell." One knows what she meant, but a soldier in the trenches would have known only the hell.

James, the artist, knew perfectly how to express the helpless anxiety of the noncombatant when, as in the following passage, he forgets the business of justifying his own situation:

The long hot July 1st of '63, on which the huge battle of Gettysburg had begun, could really be—or rather couldn't possibly not be—a scrap of concrete experience for any group of united persons, New York cousins and all, who, in a Newport garden, restlessly strolling, sitting, neither daring quite to move nor quite to rest, quite to go in or quite to stay out, actually *listened* together, in their almost ignobly safe stillness, as to the boom of far away guns.

I like to compare this description with that of another noncombatant and lifelong friend of James, the young Henry Adams, who recorded his elated reaction to the long-awaited Northern victories when news of them reached him across the Atlantic in his father's legation in London:

Life never could know more than a single such climax. In that form education reached its limits. As the first great blows began to fall, one curled up in bed in the silence of night, to listen with incredulous hope. As the huge masses struck, one after another, with the precision of machinery, the opposing mass, the world shivered. Such development of power was unknown. The magnificent resistance and the return shocks heightened the suspense. During the July days Londoners were stupid with unbelief. They were learning from the Yankees how to fight.

The time that may have been hardest for James, as a noncombatant, was when the war was all over, and his surviving friends returned, battle-scarred and decorated, from scenes of carnage to attract the admiration of applauding young women. To be a "man," a man like his friends, the future Justice Holmes and the future Harvard Law School luminary John Chipman Gray, did one have to have been a warrior? Well, at least one could look like one. James, in the three decades that followed the war, seemed bent on assuming such a stance. He adopted a stern and robust air, quite different from that of the pale, sensitive, intellectual seventeen-year-old painted in Newport by John Lafarge. An observer of him in London, in the early postwar years, described him, with his well-trimmed silken beard, as "an Elizabethan sea captain," and we can see, years later, in a photograph taken on a beach in Suffolk, hand on hip, feet apart, that he was "an imposing man whose solid body and distinctive head contributed to his being a presence," as stated in Leon Edel's *Henry James: A Life.*

He developed a lifelong enthusiasm for books on soldiers and fighting, and his library was filled with the memoirs of the marshals of Napoleon, whose identity he assumed in a wandering, irrational memorandum dictated on his deathbed. To rectify any confusion of a pursuit of the arts with passive, uncompetitive behavior, he would often equate his own desire for success and fame as a writer with the martial glories of old empires. He wrote to his mother from Rome: "It is time I should rend the veil from the ferocious ambition which has always *couvé* beneath a tranquil exterior; which enabled me to support unrecorded physical misery in my younger years: and which is perfectly confident in accomplishing serious things." And to his brother William: "If I keep along here patiently I rather think I shall become a (sufficiently) great man."

But there was still a hitch. Didn't a true man have to have a mate? A wife or a mistress or even an adored but unattainable beauty? And James in all his years was never associated with any woman save on terms of friendship. Nor is there even a reference in all his writing to the female body as a sex object. The women in his fiction may be brilliantly alive, but they are always fully dressed. The only descriptions of nudity are of young males, and they contain a distinct erotic note. Here is one from *Notes of a Son and Brother:*

> It was the real thing, the gage of a great future, when I one morning found my companions of the larger, the serious studio inspired to splendid performance by the beautiful young manly form of our cousin Gus Barker, then on a vivid little dash of a visit to us and who, perched on a pedestal and divested of every garment, was the gayest as well as the neatest of models.

Of course, the word *gay* didn't have its current meaning, but its use here may be a hint of it. And now I quote from *Italian Hours.* Half a dozen young boys are playing in a square in Torcello. They seemed to James "the handsomest little brats in the world, and each was furnished with a pair of eyes that could only have signified the protest of nature against the meanness of fortune. They were very nearly as naked as savages." One small boy seemed "the most expressively beautiful creature I had ever looked upon. He had a smile to make Correggio sigh in the grave. . . . Verily nature is still at odds with propriety. . . . I shall always remember with infinite tender conjecture, as the years roll by, this little unlettered Eros of the Adriatic Strand."

Yet prior to the time, when, in his sixties, James began to receive young male worshippers at Lamb House and address to them letters of the warmest and most tactile affection, there is not a jot of evidence that he harbored or implemented homosexual leanings. If he had them—and everything points to this, as such inclinations are not apt to be born in old age (though it is possible)—he also had them under rigid control. I believe that he shared society's prejudice against homosexuals, the popular version of whom as effeminate creatures would have certainly clashed with his own concern about appearing and *being* a man. He did not have to feel guilty about any of his own fantasies or desires, as such would have been shameful only if acted upon. He was always socially conventional; he described Oscar Wilde, even before the scandal of his trials, as an "unclean beast." In a day when buggery was a crime punishable with jail and hard labor many inverts may have taken the same course. They could have regarded their temptations as the work of the devil, and their resistance as a triumph over nature.

The repression of homosexual urges, however, did not create heterosexual ones, and the problem of explaining why a virile male did not desire a female remained. Some critics have tried to see in James's devotion to his first cousin Minnie Temple evidence of an incipient romance, but I agree with the more general conclusion that his close ties with her were protected from any expectations of romance by their kinship and by her fatal illness. She realized her true function in his life by dying and giving him a model for Isabel Archer and Milly Theale. The ancient way of seeming a man without having a woman was in the church: to be a militant and powerful priest, a Richelieu, but this was not open to James, a person of no great religious conviction. He could, however, build the life of the writer into a kind of monasticism, with the theory that women, in any role but that of mother, sister, or friend, might dangerously tap the vital energy of the artist. Lancelot was not the knight he had been after he succumbed to Guinevere. This theory of the vital power of virginity, or at least of chastity, James incorporated in *The Lesson of the Master,* in which a young novelist heeds the advice of an older one who has succumbed to the need of writing best-sellers to support a wife and family, and adopts the single life.

Of course, this was nonsense, and James must have known it. Two of his favorite authors, Hawthorne and Browning, had written their greatest works while happily married. But it fitted the picture of the great man dedicated solely to a great work, and it found an easy acceptance among his friends and admirers.

As he aged and became famous, he was able to be more relaxed about his masculine posture. He was still a great man to all the younger ones who gathered around him—Hugh Walpole, Percy Lubbock, Gaillard Lapsley, Jonathan Sturges, Moreton Fullerton, Howard Sturgis—no matter how freely he hugged them and patted their backs and shoulders and expressed his love in the warmest terms. Some of them had no shame of their same-sex inclinations and gave easy vent to them; one of them, Walpole, is supposed even to have propositioned the Master. But James was never ready for anything like that. He limited himself strictly to what Arthur Benson in his secret journal, writing of James's "power of receiving caresses," termed "the slobbering osculations of elderly men with false teeth."

One may be glad that he even had that.

Edith Wharton

EDITH WHARTON led a highly ordered and disciplined life, divided neatly but rigorously among her principal activities: the writing of beautiful books, the cultivation of beautiful gardens, the visitation of beautiful places, and the collection . . . well, not perhaps of beautiful people but of those compatible souls who shared her love of beautiful things. All this emerges strongly enough from her books, though her readers may at the same time glean something of the cost to the author of what her friend Henry James called "the wear and tear of discrimination."

The married years of her life, almost thirty of them, were constantly disturbed by an irritable and ultimately almost insane husband, Edward Wharton, who first had seemed only an amiable and easygoing if somewhat Philistine idler, but who turned in time into a bored neurotic who couldn't abide the epicene court of intellectual bachelors attracted to his wife. Edith at last, at the age of forty-seven, took refuge in a three-year clandestine love affair with Moreton Fullerton, a charming but selfish and self-centered American journalist who took maximum advantage of his fatal attraction to both sexes. Some critics, since the belated discovery of this affair, which Edith kept secret from her husband and the world, have ventured to find a warmer, more human note in the fiction she wrote after it, but I have been unable to perceive any difference, and Edith herself, though she maintained a friendship with Fullerton after the bitter end of the affair, wrote him that she would have been better off had she never met him.

There is no question that Edith felt that she had sadly missed in life the emotional fulfillment of an open and happily shared love. In a letter to her French translator, Charles DuBos, she wrote of the bliss of a mutual passion that did not have to be hidden from the crowd. But if there were substitutes for such a good fortune, she certainly had them. She had had to work for them, of course. She had had to free herself from the stuffy confines of a proper lady's life in the old Knickerbocker society of New York; she had had to learn languages and adapt herself to the more sophisticated circles of London and Paris; she had had to carve out for herself a solid and enduring niche in the international world of letters. That she knew she had done all these things, and done them, so to speak, alone, she made clear in her restrained—but penetrable to the careful reader—memoirs.

But the mind that helped her to achieve her goals had to be a very sharp one, at times perhaps almost too sharp, and she was always vividly aware of the small-mindedness and meanness of those who had been obstacles in her way, and piteous, if rather scornfully so, of those who had inadequately tried and woefully failed to win what she had won. I found, in compiling an anthology of what I deemed the finest samples of her incomparable prose, a marked emphasis in them of the sorry plight of the dilettante, the half-liver, the man or woman who lets form take precedence over matter and possessiveness precedence over love. She knew only too well what her own dangers had been.

And so in her many novels and stories we feel we are in the grip of a woman of the highest intellect and finest taste who has fought a long and successful battle against the imps of vulgarity and complacency. What she found particularly sad in the world she observed so keenly, and so pathetically different from the fullness of her own life, were persons who strived and lived and hated with only half the energy they could have summoned to cope with the emotion or activity in question. If this makes the following excerpts from her work sound too negative, remember that Wharton's criticisms are founded on her passionate belief that life should and could be a vital and wonderful experience and that she is always doing her bit to try to make it so.

Perhaps the least attractive aspect of Wharton's personality as it comes through to us in her fiction is to be found in the harshness of her criticism of her native land. It should, of course, be remembered that it was a very different America from the one we live in today and that it contained all the things from which she believed she had to flee to recreate her true self. Here is how she saw a New England summer resort, in *Madame de Treymes:*

"And then your married sister's spending her summers at—where is it?— The Kittawittnay House at Lake Pohunc—"

A vision of earnest young women in Shetland shawls, with spectacles and thin knobs of hair, eating blueberry pie at unwholesome hours in a shingled dining-room on a bare New England hilltop, rose pallidly between Durham and the verdant brightness of the Champs-Elysées.

And here is the New York poor relative, in *The House of Mirth:*

Grace Stepney was an obscure cousin, of adaptable manners and vicarious interests, who "ran in" to sit with Mrs. Peniston when Lily dined out too continuously, who played bezique, picked up dropped stitches, read out the deaths from the Times, and sincerely admired the purple satin drawing-room curtains, the Dying Gladiator in the window and the seven-by-five painting of Niagara which represented the one artistic excess of Mr. Peniston's temperate career.

And, in *Madame de Treymes,* the contrast of New York to Paris:

His European visits were infrequent enough to have kept unimpaired the freshness of his eye, and he was always struck anew by the vast and consummately ordered spectacle of Paris: by its look of having been boldly and deliberately planned for the enjoyment of life instead of being forced into grudging concessions by the festive instincts, or barricading itself against them in unenlightened ugliness, like his own lamentable New York.

Yet beautiful things could be born in America and even developed there. Lily Bart in *The House of Mirth* was one:

Everything about her was at once vigorous and exquisite, at once strong and fine. He had a confused sense that she must have cost a great deal to make, that a great many dull and ugly people must, in some mysterious way, have been sacrificed to produce her.

Nor was it always the fault of the intellectually underprivileged that they were so benighted, as seen in *The Fruit of the Tree:*

It seemed to her that the tragic crises in wedded life usually turned on the stupidity of one of the two concerned; and of the two victims of such a catastrophe she felt most for the one whose limitations had probably brought it about. After all there could be no imprisonment as cruel as that of being bounded by a hard small nature. Not to be penetrable at all points to the shifting lights, the wandering music of the world—she could imagine no physical disability as cramping as that. How the little parched soul, in solitary confinement for life, must pine and dwindle in the blind cranny of self-love!

Writers and Personality

But she was always severe on the dilettante. She writes in *The Reef:*

> In the first years of her marriage the sober symmetry of Givre [the American expatriate family's chateau] had suggested only her husband's neatly balanced mind. It was a mind, she soon learned, contentedly absorbed in formulating the conventions of the unconventional. West Fifty-fifth Street was no more conscientiously concerned than Givre with the momentous question of "what people did"; it was only the type of deed investigated that was different. Mr. Leath collected his social instances with the same seriousness and patience as his snuff-boxes. He exacted a rigid conformity to his rules of non-conformity, and his skepticism had the absolute accent of a dogma. He even cherished certain exceptions to his rules as the book collector prizes a "defective" first edition. The Protestant church-going of Anna's parents had provoked his gentle sarcasm; but he prided himself on his mother's devoutness, because Madame de Chantelle, in embracing her second husband's creed, had become part of a society which still observes the outward rites of piety.

Wharton could be gentle, however, with fools, as seen in *Xingu:*

> Mrs. Ballinger is one of the ladies who pursue Culture in bands, as though it were dangerous to meet alone.

And sympathetic with those who really tried, as in, for example, *The Age of Innocence:*

> Something he knew he had missed: the flower of life. But he thought of it now as a thing so unattainable and improbable that to have repined would have been like despairing because one had not drawn the first prize in a lottery. There were a hundred million tickets in *his* lottery, and there was only one prize; the chances had been too decidedly against him. When he thought of Ellen Olenska it was abstractedly, serenely, as one might think of some imaginary beloved in a book or a picture: she had become the composite vision of all that he had missed.

But there was always that side of Edith Wharton that knew when it was necessary, or at least wise, to bow to the unbeatable aspects of a conventional society. Ellen Olenska in *The Age of Innocence* knows from her ean observations that there is no place where an adulterous couple can escape with total freedom the withering eyes of an outraged society.

"Is it your idea that I should live with you as your mistress—since I can't be your wife?" she asked. . . .

"I want—I want somehow to get away with you into a world where words like that—categories like that—won't exist."

She drew a deep breath that ended in another laugh. "Oh, my dear— where is that country? Have you ever been there?" she asked, and as he remained silently dumb she went on: "I know so many who've tried to find it; and, believe me, they all got out by mistake at wayside stations; at places like Boulogne, or Pisa, or Monte Carlo—and it wasn't at all different from the old world they'd left, but only rather smaller and dingier and more promiscuous."

Pierre Corneille

ORNEILLE HAD THE LUCK to be born in just the right nation and at just the right time to suit his temperament, for he was a passionate royalist who had no quarrel either with the boast of Louis XIV, "L'état c'est moi," or with that monarch's incessant and aggressive warfare. To Winston Churchill, in his biography of his great ancestor, Marlborough, the Sun King may have been reduced to the status of international pest, but to Corneille he was the ultimately glorious symbol of Gallic superiority. He describes him in *Attila* in the obvious guise of the rising king of the Gauls:

> Mais si de nos devins l'oracle n'est point faux,
> Sa grandeur doit atteindre aux degrés les plus hauts;
> Et de ses successeurs l'empire inébranlable
> Sera de siècle en siècle enfin si redoutable,
> Qu'un jour toute la terre en recevra des lois,
> Ou tremblera du moins au nom de leur François.

The essence of Corneille's personality is conveyed in his worship of doughty warriors dedicated to the military aggrandizement of their country. What, he is always asking, can be nobler than to be respected, even to be feared? It is true that he started his career with a regrettable clash with Cardinal Richelieu over the latter's unreasonable and perhaps jealous antagonism to *Le Cid,* but he was quick to placate that all-powerful statesman with his dedication to him of *Horace* in terms fulsomely flattering even in that knee-bending day. "C'est là que lisant sur son visage ce qui lui plaît et ce qui ne lui plaît pas, nous nous instruisons avec certitude de ce qui est bon et ce qui est mauvais, et tirons des règles infaillibles de ce qu'il faut suivre et ce qu'il faut éviter; c'est là que j'ai souvent appris en deux heures ce que mes livres n'eussent pu m'apprendre en dix ans."

Richeleiu, after all, Corneille was now quite willing to concede, had founded the state that Louis XIV would bring to its zenith, by centralizing all political power in the hands of an absolute monarch whose armies would dominate the European scene. Corneille did not live to see the defeats that would darken the end of the Sun King's reign; it was all glory while he lived, though he came in his old age to appreciate some of the bitterness aroused by unbridled despotism.

Horace is the purest expression of Corneille's early tolerance of even the goriest aspects of embattled patriotism. His Roman eponymous hero, returning the victor in the duel on the outcome of which the fates of Rome and Alba had been staked and in which his sister's fiancé, an Alban, has been slain, is so horrified to hear her curse her native city that he slaughters her on the spot. Neither he nor his old father feels that the unfortunate woman has been unjustly treated. She has cursed her fatherland, which merits death. Horace, Senior, a fearsome patriot who has, just before, wanted to exercise his right to kill his son on hearing the false rumor that the latter has fled the field of combat, now simply finds it wrong that a son of his should have been the one to wreak justice on his daughter.

> Son crime, quoique énorme et digne du trépas,
> Etait mieux impuni que puni par ton bras.

And his son never apologizes for the murder, even suggesting that he be executed for it, but only because it is unlikely that he will ever again repeat so glorious a feat as winning the duel for Rome and because lesser heroic acts in the future may tarnish his fame: "La mort seule aujourd'hui peut conserver ma gloire."

The only higher thing than dying for the state is dying for God. In *Polyeucte* the hero of the drama's title rushes, immediately after his baptism as a Christian, with an exalted joy to destroy the pagan idols in the Roman temple, an act for which he knows the penalty is death which he cheerfully accepts. If the most excruciating tortures should precede his execution, so much the better. He cries:

> Non, non, persecutez,
> Et soyez l'instrument de nos félicités;
> Celle d'un vrai chrétien n'est que dans les souffrances;
> Les plus cruels tourments lui sont des recompenses.
> Dieu, qui rend le centuple aux bonnes actions,
> Pour comble donne encore les persecutions.

There may even be a touch of Louis XIV in a god who now takes precedence of all earthly authority. The hero states:

> Je n'adore qu'un Dieu, maître de l'univers,
> Sous qui tremble le ciel, la terre et les enfers;
> Un Dieu qui, nous aimant d'une amour infinie,
> Voulût mourir pour nous avec ignominie.

Note that all tremble at his name. To cause fear as well as awe is the dream of the Corneille hero.

And yet as his long and successful career drew to a close, Corneille became more and more conscious that a hero—a true hero—may have trouble with the state no matter how faithfully he serves the master. Indeed, there is such a thing as serving too well; an absolute sovereign may take jealous offense at a general who is too successful; he may even come to fear and hate him. He may come to wish him assassinated. That is what happens to Suréna, the hero of a final tragedy of the same name. He has done too well by his ungrateful Parthian king, and he has only this to say:

> Je lui dois en sujet tout mon sang, tout mon bien;
> Mais si je lui dois tout, mon coeur ne lui doit rien,
> Et n'en reçois de lois que comme autant d'outrages,
> Comme autant d'attentats sur de plus doux hommages.

We have come a long way from the blind loyalty of Horace.

Henry Adams

ENRY ADAMS'S sharply defined personality expresses itself vividly in the two books on which his reputation most solidly rests: *The Education of Henry Adams* and *Mont-Saint-Michel and Chartres.* The first is an autobiography—or what is essentially one despite the gaps of the unsaid—and the second ostensibly a travel book in which a supposed uncle explains the French thirteenth century to nieces, so the reader is inevitably exposed to some personal visions of the storyteller. In *The Education* Adams makes some effort to draw apart from the reader by referring to himself in the third person, and in *Mont-Saint-Michel* by adopting the role of uncle, but we have always a clear view of this very busy, neatly attired, eminently curious little gentlemen, poking his walking stick into every hole and cranny that he passes, ferreting out the most extraordinary things, passionately determined never to abandon his search for a solution to the riddle of the universe, no matter how bleak such a solution may prove to be.

He is grave; he is humorous; he never loses his head or his temper; he is always polite, always a gentleman. If his eye is merciless, his heart is kind. And he never bores us, for he cannot bear to be bored himself.

Critics have often called him falsely modest. He constantly says that he is uneducated, though he received as fine an education as his world could provide, both in books and experience. He has this modest assessment of his value to journalism: "The enormous mass of his misinformation accumulated in ten years of a normal life could always be worked off on a helpless public, in diluted doses, if one could but secure a table in the corner of a newspaper office." Yet his articles in the *North American Review* are still read today. And he claims that the course in medieval history which he taught at Harvard brought little or nothing to his students despite their vociferous claims to the contrary.

To designate these statements, and many like them, as falsely modest, or even modest, is to misread them. What Adams is claiming is that education as it existed in his youth *everywhere* failed to prepare men in how to handle the differences that separated the nineteenth century from its predecessor. Every man knew, of course, that changes, great changes, had occurred. What they utterly failed to comprehend, Adams claimed, was just how great those changes were: that a seemingly impassable gulf now yawned between the America of President Grant, Commodore Vanderbilt, and Jay Gould and the America of Washington, Jefferson, and John Adams. Only half jokingly he averred that the contrast might be enough to disprove the theory of evolution.

He might have called his autobiography *The Education of a Generation*. Far from being modest he even took pride in the slight superiority that his recognition of his own ignorance gave him over those who deemed themselves adequately equipped to deal with the modern world. The current of the time was to be *his* current, he boldly asserted: "He was fifty years in advance of his time." But long before he came to this understanding, back when, at age thirty, in 1868, he returned to America after seven years in our London embassy, he had found a strange country. "Not a Polish Jew fresh from Warsaw or Cracow—not a furtive Yacoob or Ysaak reeking of the Ghetto, snarling a weird Yiddish to the officers of the customs—but had a keener instinct, an intenser energy and a freer hand than he—American of Americans, with Heaven knew how many Puritans and Patriots behind him, and an education that had cost a civil war" (*The Education*).

But if Adams considered himself ill equipped to handle a changed American he had no better opinion of those of his contemporaries who did not deem themselves so handicapped. Writing to Henry James about the latter's biography of William Wetmore Story he observed: "The painful truth is that all of my generation . . . were in actual fact only one mind and name; the individual was a facet of Boston. . . . We knew nothing—no! but really nothing of the world. One cannot exaggerate the profundity of ignorance of Story becoming a sculptor, or in Sumner becoming a statesman, or Emerson in becoming a philosopher" ("Letters of Henry Adams").

But if the "gentlemen" of the old school failed as leaders, what of those rising from the depths? Adams had even less hope for them. The so-called robber barons, the lords of railroads, oil, and steel, he deemed actually worse. With them the making of money was all. He said of the typical financial tycoon: "The amusement of the pursuit was all the amusement he got from it; he had no use of wealth. Jim Fisk alone seemed to know what he wanted; Jay Gould never did" (*The Education*). Such men didn't even know when they were bored!

Adams was one of the first to perceive that the danger of a laisser-faire economy to democratic government was not only a present danger but a constantly recurring one as well. In 1870 he wrote an account of the vicious attempt of Gould and Fisk to corner the gold market by bribing men close to Grant not to let the government buy gold. The plot failed, but Adams's warning that such things were bound to come back makes grim reading for those who have endured the financial scandals of 2003:

> For the first time since the creation of these enormous corporate bodies, one of them has shown its power for mischief, and has proved itself able to override and trample on law, custom, decency and every restraint known to society, without scruple and as yet without check. The belief is common in America that the day is at hand when corporations far greater than the Erie . . . will ultimately succeed in directing government itself. Under the American form of society no authority exists capable of effective resistance. The national government, in order to deal with the corporations, must assume powers refused to it by its fundamental law—and then is exposed to the chance of forming an absolute central government which sooner or later is likely to fall into the hands it is struggling to escape, and thus destroy the limits of its power only to make corruption omnipotent. ("The New York Gold Conspiracy")

And has not all that happened since? In the decades following 1870 the giant corporations were created: The Standard Oil Company and the steel and railroad empires consolidated by J. P. Morgan who notoriously deemed himself the equal of an American president. The government, at first powerless to control them, at length, under the two Roosevelt presidents, assumed powers that for many years a Supreme Court pronounced forbidden by fundamental law. An altered court finally changed this, and the government has become what, at least to Adams in 1870, would have been regarded as an absolute central one. And even a conservative in 2003 would have to admit that the Republican administration of George W. Bush favors the great corporations. Indeed, it almost boasts of doing so.

Critics have also taken Adams to task for never having accepted a political appointment, for sitting, so to speak, on the sidelines and pitching bottles at the umpire. Justice Oliver Wendell Holmes observed that calling on his friend Adams after a hard day's work on the court and hearing him play the cynical old cardinal who could pull everything apart, was not always what a tired judge needed. This was the natural reaction of a man deeply involved in trying to work out problems that his friend simply deplored. But that need not hinder us from being entranced by what Adams wrote. He liked to say that that he had never taken a government position because no president had ever asked him to. It was like him to expect that any such bid would come from the White House itself. But his real reason was that he did not believe that any man could induce either the legislative or executive branches of the government in the last four decades of the nineteenth century to take any significant steps in reform. He could only record what he so carefully observed, and such a record might one day be of value to those who *could* act.

But there was another side of Adams that comes out strongly in his tight and seamless prose: his aesthetic side. "He would rather, as choice, have gone back to the east, if it were only to sleep forever in the trade-winds under the southern stars, wandering over the dark purple ocean, with its purple sense of solitude and void" (*The Education*). In *Mont-Saint-Michel* one feels his yearning for the unity of a simpler day, a single faith, for the consolation of the Virgin as reflected in the blue glass of Chartres, for the absence of all the vulgarity in the harsh modern world. But where is that unity now? He can only leave the Virgin in her majesty "with her three great prophets on either hand, as calm and confident in their own strength and in God's providence as they were when Saint Louis was born, but looking down from a deserted heaven, into an empty church, on a dead faith."

Perhaps we see Adams most clearly in the passage in *The Education* in which he describes a visit to his wife's tomb in Rock Creek Park over which Saint-Gaudens's brooding, sexless, robed figure is seated, in deep contemplation, and comments on the remarks of visitors.

As Adams sat there numbers of people came, for the figure seemed to have become a tourist fashion, and all wanted to know its meaning. Most took it for a portrait-statue, and the remnant were vacant-minded in the absence of a personal guide. None felt what would have been a nursery instinct to a Hindu baby or a Japanese jinricksha-runner. The only exceptions were the clergy who taught a lesson even deeper. One after another brought companions there, and apparently fascinated by their own reflection, broke out passionately against the expression they felt in the figure of despair, of atheism, of denial. Like the others the priest saw only what he brought. Like all great artists, Saint-Gaudens held up the mirror and no more. The American layman had lost sight of ideals; the American priest had lost sight of faith. Both were more American than the old, half-witted soldiers who denounced the wasting, on a mere grave, of money which should have been given for drink.

Prosper Merimée

ROSPER MERIMÉE, like Flaubert, believed in the complete suppression of the author's personality in any work of fiction, though he would occasionally interrupt a story, like a lecturer pausing to answer a question from his audience, to explain where he was heading or what he chose to omit. But aside from such editorial footnotes the text itself of each tale is bare of the writer's comments or appraisals. The characters stand clear and the events are graphically delineated: the reader may draw his own conclusions as to what approval, disapproval, or indifference should be meted out to their moral choices.

Yet a glimpse of the essential Merimée can be gleaned from the pages of his two major novels: *Chronique du règne de Charles IX* and *Colomba*. In both tales we are confronted with violence and slaughter: in the first with the religious wars of the French sixteenth century and the Massacre of Saint Bartholomew, and in the second with the blood feuds of post-Napoleonic Corsica. It is very evident that the author, a gentleman of high learning, polite sophistication, and perhaps post-Waterloo disillusionment, harbors a distinct sympathy for the brave embattled men of eras less inhibited than his own, that he admires those who would fight a duel to the death over the merest pin prick to their honor, or wreak a terrible revenge for a death in the family, if murder be even faintly suspected, on the first person accused. One feels Merimée's pleasure even in bandits as men not shackled with all the effeminizing "don'ts" of his own era; for all the evil that they did, they yet had something that the noodles of his own age lacked. He must have fantasized that it might have been exhilarating to have lived in the Paris of Catherine de' Medici or in the Corsica of the "good old days," even if one risked dying at a sword's point. Indeed, wasn't the risk half the energizing thrill?

But Merimée was far too intelligent, too worldly wise, and even too agnostic to believe for a moment that contemporary life would really be improved by the revival of religious strife or blood feuds. His two best novels make perfectly evident what hash the rivalry between fanatical Catholics and Protestants made of France and how sombre an atmosphere the generations of family hatred created in Corsica. In *Colomba* the two points of view—for and against the feuds—are fairly delineated by the two principal female characters: the fierce but fascinating Colomba, who remorselessly drives her brother to avenge his father's death, even adding to his fire false evidence of the continuing hostility of their enemy, and her brother's beloved, the English Miss Nevil, who finds the Corsicans romantically Byronic in their violence but wishes to curb them to civilized British restraints. It is obvious that Miss Nevil is a wiser guide than Colomba, but it is equally obvious that the latter is possessed of all her creator's heart and that the victory of Miss Nevil, who is something of a namby-pamby, is only of the mind.

Only once in the *Chronique du règne de Charles IX* does Merimée allow his own partiality to slip out. During the Massacre of Saint Bartholomew some captured Calvinists are offered their lives in return for an abjuration. One profits by this offer, "et consentit à se racheter de la mort et même des tourments par un mensonge peut-être excusable." The "peut-être" from such an agnostic as Merimée shows that to him life was not worth a lie. It was not the betrayal of a faith that bothered him; it was the abject surrender to brute force that offended his lofty gentleman's point of view. He probably admired the Duchesse de Grammont, who chose the guillotine rather than deny to the Jacobins that she had been corresponding with the emigrés.

But that personality can be shown in its very repression is brilliantly demonstrated in this passage from Walter Pater's *Miscellaneous Studies:*

> Merimée's superb self-effacement, his impersonality, is itself but an effective personal trait, and, transferred to art, becomes a markedly peculiar quality of literary beauty. For, in truth, this creature of disillusion who had no care for half-lights, and, like his creations, had no atmosphere about him, gifted as he was with pure *mind,* with the quality which secures flawless literary structure, had, on the other hand, nothing of what we call *soul* in literature:—hence, also, that singular harshness in his ideal, as if, in theological language, he were incapable of grace. He has none of those subjectivities, colorings, peculiarities of mental refraction, which necessitate *varieties* of style—could we spare such?—and render the perfections of it no merely negative qualities. There are masters of French prose whose art has begun where the art of Merimée leaves off.

George Eliot

G EORGE ELIOT, who wrote what to my mind is the greatest novel of manners of the Victorian age, *Middlemarch,* expressed in her work a personality very different from the bright and colorful scenes that she so brilliantly evoked. She allowed the deep and serious aspect of her own grave character to permeate her pages with a sometimes rather depressing effect. Consider the fate of Maggie Tulliver in *The Mill on the Floss.*

Maggie is not in love with crippled Philip Wakem, but she greatly admires his fine character, and, of course, his passion for her as well as his wealth offers her an escape from poverty and dependence. But the feud between their fathers seems a fatal bar to their union. However, she continues to see Philip clandestinely, allowing him at least to hope that she will some day be his. The fact that she conceals their meetings from her father and brother is, in her author's stern judgment, her first grave fault. Philip has sought "to overcome Maggie's true prompting against a concealment that would introduce doubleness into her own mind, and might cause misery to those who had the primary natural claim on her."

The assertion that Maggie's family have a primary claim over that of a lover of honorable intentions comes clearly from the author herself. It is a part of her formidable code of duty.

Maggie then falls in love with handsome Stephen Guest, who, though not actually engaged to her cousin, Lucy Dean, is widely regarded as Lucy's future fiancé and certainly enjoys her full and confident devotion. But Stephen returns Maggie's love, and when they have, by accident, been thrown together for a night away from their homes, they become lovers, only to find themselves caught out. Stephen offers at once to marry Maggie, but Maggie refuses him, regarding such a union as a double betrayal of Lucy and Philip. Here is how she talks to her lover:

"We can only choose whether we will indulge ourselves in the present moment, or whether we will renounce that, for the sake of obeying the divine voice within us—for the sake of being true to all the motives that sanctify our lives."

And this:

"You feel, as I do, that the real tie lies in the feelings and expectations we have raised in other minds. Else all pledges might be broken, when there was no outward penalty. There would be no such thing as faithfulness."

The choice is simplified for Maggie by the fact that marriage to Stephen would mean social acceptance, wealth, and a loving husband, and rejecting it would entail public disgrace, poverty, and lovelessness. To a George Eliot heroine, as to Corneille's hero Polyeucte, the grimmer destiny is the more attractive one.

With this great difference. Polyeucte, in braving a martyr's death, deems himself standing before the opening gates of heaven and a welcoming God. George Eliot, despite her reference to a "divine" voice within, nowhere in her fiction gives the slightest evidence of any belief in a rewarding providence. To her, duty must be performed for its own dark sake alone.

Maggie not only encounters the scorn of a condemning society; she meets her death in a flood which seems a part of her nemesis. George Eliot appears to have conceived a species of Greek tragedy in which noble characters are the victims of a rhadamanthine code of morals designed by whimsical gods, or perhaps by no gods at all. For what good does Maggie's rejection of Stephen do anyone? He will never go back to Lucy, nor will Maggie wed Philip. Her sacrifice has only increased the general woe. But George Eliot is not really so much interested in Lucy's or Philip's case; she is concerned only with Maggie's soul, even if it is consigned to extinction.

Some of this same spirit pervades George Eliot's heavily researched novel of fifteenth-century Florence, *Romola,* which even such an Eliot fan as Henry James said stank of libraries. Eliot does not go quite so far as to applaud Savonarola's public burning of books of beautiful pagan poetry and classic works of art along with the wigs and rouge pots of wealthy citizens, but I feel that she somehow shares the point of view of her saintly heroine who "is conscious of no inward collision with the strict and sombre view of pleasure which tended to repress poetry in the attempt to repress vice."

And in Eliot's *Daniel Deronda* I feel myself at last in direct opposition to the author in her treatment of the unhappy and lovely Gwendolyn Harleth and the priggish hero Deronda. Gwendolyn, I insist, is unduly scolded for a natural and essentially harmless vanity and made to fall in love with a man who considers his only duty to her that of murmuring pious homilies in her ear at dinner parties.

It is not wholly surprising, therefore, in searching a key to George Eliot's character outside her fiction, to come across this account of her by F. H. W. Myers, the author of *Human Personality and Its Survival of Bodily Death*. Walking in Cambridge on an evening of rainy May, Myers and Eliot discussed the words *God, Immortality*, and *Duty*, and Eliot pronounced with a terrible earnestness how inconceivable was the first, how unbelievable the second, and how peremptory and absolute the third:

> Never perhaps have sterner accents affirmed the sovereignty of impersonal and unrecompensing Law. I listened, and night fell; her grave, majestic countenance turned towards me like a sibyl's in the gloom; it was as though she withdrew from my grasp, one by one, the two scrolls of promise and left me the third scroll only, awful with inevitable fates. And when we stood at length and parted, amid that columnar circuit of forest trees, beneath the last twilight of starlight skies, I seemed to be gazing, like Titus at Jerusalem, on vacant seats and empty halls—on a sanctuary with no presence to hallow it, and heaven left lonely of a God.

Marcel Proust

I T MIGHT APPEAR that Marcel Proust is revealing all the facets of his personality in *Remembrance of Things Past,* for his narrator appears to be none other than himself and is even, in *The Captive,* given the name Marcel. Furthermore Marcel's life is almost parallel to Proust's own: both are contemporaries and bachelors who frequent the same stylish society; Marcel's childhood Combray is Proust's Illers, and Proust enters the novel himself to inform us that Swann, the father of the boy Marcel's girlfriend, Gilberte, is modeled on Charles Haas, whom he knew as a young man. But there are three marked discrepancies between Marcel and his creator: Marcel is not a Jew, not a snob, and not a homosexual, and the reader can easily infer that Proust was all three.

We suspect that Proust was Jewish—of course, it is well known to every reader today—because of his intense interest in the subject. A great deal is made of Swann's Jewishness; he has basically turned away from his racial and religious heritage and has scaled the loftiest social altitudes, hurdling walls of anti-Semitism. He is the only Jew to be accepted by the Jockey Club; he is a friend of royalty and can weekend with the Comte de Paris; he is the darling of the little group that hovers around the Duchesse de Guermantes who reigns over the Faubourg Saint-Germain. Yet his sympathy for the condemned officer in the Dreyfus case reignites his racial loyalty, and he throws away his whole social position by marrying a demimondaine whom he has ceased to love, presumably to legitimize their daughter. As he ages his facial features become more and more Hebraic, as if to reclaim an estray. One is sure that Proust had meditated deeply on the problems of being Jewish in an anti-Semitic society, particularly for those who are not attracted by their heritage but are too finely proud to deny it.

Some critics have denied that Proust was a snob because he delineates so sharply and meticulously the pettiness and meanness of many of his titled characters. But that is because nothing escaped his all observing eye. It is entirely possible for even the most distinguished writers to be dazzled by the society that they so adroitly satirize: Balzac and Thackeray may suffice as examples. Edith Wharton wrote in her memoirs that she never met Proust or even wished to, after being told "that the only people who really interested him were dukes and duchesses" (*The Writing of Fiction*). She concluded that his "greatness lay in his art, his incredible littleness in the quality of his social admirations." Proust may have tried to justify his enthusiasm for the titles and trappings of the French nobility by claiming that they evoked in his mind wonderful pictures of the history of France, but his long and vivid descriptions of the parties of the Guermantes and their sort are witness to a zeal that is not wholly scholarly.

There are even passages in *Remembrance* in which Marcel seems to be sharing the fantasies of his author. Here is a sample of what he is thinking in the little train that bears him from Balbec to Doncière. He is studying a fellow passenger:

> The lady wore an air of extreme dignity; and as I, for my part, was inwardly aware that I was invited, two days hence, to the house of the celebrated Mme. Verdurin, at the terminal point of the little railway line, that at an intermediate station I was awaited by Robert de Saint-Loup, and that a little further on I would have given great pleasure to Mme. de Cambremer by going to stay at Feterne, my eyes sparkled with irony as I gazed at this self-important lady who seemed to think that, because of her elaborate attire, the feathers in her hat, her *Revue des Deux Mondes,* she was a more considerable person than myself.

For what purpose was this passage inserted in the novel? To make fun of Marcel? But he is not anywhere else made to seem an ass. It seems, more simply, to represent a mood of the author's.

Marcel is not only represented as "straight"; he is one of the few characters who is not, even occasionally, homosexual. He shares this classification with Swann, though both are tortured with jealousy over the lesbian tastes of their mistresses. Few characters in the novel escape being brushed, one way or another, by what we designate by the coined adjective "same sex." Charlus, Morel, Saint-Loup, Odette, Albertine, the Prince de Guermantes, Vinteuil's daughter, and many others are all either totally or partially homosexual. That Proust was, too, is evident not only from his obsession with the subject and his inclination to find it in everyone, but in his conception of Marcel's affair with Albertine. His love for her is born when Doctor Cottard points out to him that when she is dancing with another girl they press their breasts together for mutual sexual satisfaction. This should alert the reader to the fact that this will be no common-or-garden boy-girl romance. We then learn that Albertine is allowed to stay over night with him in the apartment of his utterly respectable parents, a hospitality which would have been limited to his male friends. And finally, if we wonder why, as Marcel cannot live without knowing what she is up to every minute she is not with him, he doesn't marry her, the answer must be that he cannot marry a man.

Proust's theory that jealousy is the principal generator of true love has been taken seriously by generations of critics. But what he is really doing is universalizing the case history of a neurasthenic: himself. Of course it is true that jealousy plays a heavy role in French nineteenth- and early-twentieth-century fiction, whose heroes are largely of the upper or upper middle class. In a *désoeuvré* society in which the men are primarily interested in the slaughter of animals and the pursuit of women, analysis of the relation between the sexes can become a kind of obsession. The woman who becomes a gentleman's mistress must, at least until he terminates the affair, be absolutely faithful. He can hardly bear the idea that she can have ever belonged to another man, and if this is the case, which it naturally almost always is, there must be no taint left of previous loves. Even a writer as broad-minded as Anatole France has the hero of his most famous novel, *The Red Lily,* break off with the woman he adores because he discovers that she has had an affair, even though terminated, too soon before the date of their meeting.

The narrator Marcel is so interested in homosexuality, though ostensibly not an invert himself, that he will go to any length to spy upon people engaged in the act. It is certainly an aspect of Proust's personality that he saw no objection to this, for there is not the faintest touch of author disapproval in the passage in which Marcel hoists himself up to peer through a transom window at the amorous activities of the Baron de Charlus and the tailor Jupien. Edith Wharton was disgusted:

> There is one deplorable page where the hero and narrator, with whose hyper-sensitiveness a hundred copious and exquisite passages have acquainted us, describes with complacency how he has deliberately hidden himself to spy on an unedifying scene. (*The Writing of Fiction*)

Just as an undue value has been placed on Proust's theories of love and jealousy, so has his concept of the capture of past time been blown up into a new philosophy of the role of art in life. Yet what is this concept but his recognition of the well-known fact that some seemingly unrelated incident, a metallic sound or the taste of a cracker, identical with a sound or taste that we recall from long ago, can suddenly evoke in an appropriately sensitive mind the whole picture of a bygone world? Marcel enjoys this experience on different occasions, but it is not through them that he can tell us the story of Swann's love, which he gets through hearsay, or the innumerable other incidents that make up the novel which he has observed at first hand and remembers only too well without the aid of the prompting incidents.

No, Proust was not a great psychiatrist or a great philosopher. He simply wrote a novel of manners. But it just so happens that it was the greatest novel of manners ever written.

Scott Fitzgerald and
Ernest Hemingway

T HE GREAT GATSBY glows with the reflection of the personality of
F. Scott Fitzgerald. It is all there: the casual disillusionment with
the meanness and hypocrisy of the everyday world, and the rising
above it with the aid of wit, nonchalance, fatalism, alcohol, constant partying, temperate friendships, and temperate love affairs—but above
all with the aid of a strong innate sense of personal superiority. Yet nothing
can alter the fact that this hedonism in Fitzgerald is always darkened by the
sense of its briefness. Age looms: "Thirty—the promise of a decade of loneliness, the thinning list of single men to know, a thinning brief-case of enthusiasm, thinning hair." And all the glittering things: the beautiful houses of the
rich on Long Island Sound, the beautiful women who live in them with the
chink of money in their very laughter, the beautifully attired men who ride
to hounds and drive shining yellow Rolls-Royces, the gleaming white yachts
—what are they but a mirage, and what is a mirage but the only thing to live
for?

Jay Gatsby, the hero, if heroes there be in Fitzgerald's world, is a gangster
who has made a fortune by violence, presumably even by murder, but he has
a gallant war record and is capable of real passion. His strong and enduring
love for Daisy Buchanan appears in some way to redeem him, if he be indeed
redeemable, and his taking seriously the American dream of the good life
based on an abundance of material things seems to elevate him over the triv-
iality and selfishness of the other characters, including the narrator Nick. And
he proves himself capable of one noble act: he takes upon himself the guilt
of a hit-and-run driver though the person actually at the lethal wheel of his
car was his beloved Daisy, and he pays for this with his life at the hands of the

victim's husband. Gatsby's great virtue in the eyes of his creator is that he has style.

Yet even Gatsby in the end has a vision of the futility of his dream. As Alfred Kazin has put it in *On Native Grounds:*

> It was as if Fitzgerald, the playboy, moving with increasing despair through this trial world of Gatsby's, had reached that perfect moment, before the break of darkness and death, when the mind does really absolutely know itself—the moment when only those who never lived by Gatsby's great illusion, lived by the tinsel and the glamor, can feel the terrible force of self-betrayal.

Fitzgerald's prose is as fine as any written in the twentieth century. The writing of beautiful fiction must have been the one thing that he could cling to in his world of inevitable disillusionment. To quote Kazin again: he brought "a major art to a minor vision of life."

Ernest Hemingway believed that life offered larger opportunities than did Fitzgerald, but they were strictly limited in number and quality. Infinite satisfaction was to be had in acts of great courage, in big-game hunting, in the study of bull fighting, and in love. For what Sir Walter Scott called "a laggard in love and a dastard in war" Hemingway had only contempt, but in reading him I always have the uneasy feeling that he included most men (he was easier on women) in one or the other of these two detested categories. For his standards were grimly high.

Francis Macomber redeems himself from a life of shameful timidity in the last minute of his existence. His "short happy life" is ended by a bullet shot by a wife who cannot bear to have him emerge from the scathing limelight of her scorn, but he dies in the joyful realization that he has made up for his cowardly flight from a wounded lion by bravely facing and killing a charging water buffalo.

In *The Sun Also Rises* the character whom Hemingway most admires is the toreador Romero who risks his life happily by keeping so close to the raging bull that they almost seem to touch. He is not only the perfect performing artist; he is also the perfect man. Jake, the narrator, and his friend Harvey Stone have no opportunities for heroism, but they achieve the author's approval by their love of fishing and bull fighting, as does the promiscuous Lady Brett for realizing that she is a bad influence on the young toreador and giving him up. But what is most illuminating as to Hemingway's attitude toward this little group of Americans and English who go to Pamplona is his treatment of Robert Cohn.

I think of Cohn as representing all that Hemingway regards as least capable of any of the grand moments of life—probably a large section of mankind. He has made him a Jew, a fact invidiously and constantly commented on by all the other characters in the book, which may indicate prejudice in the author but more probably is intended to explain Cohn's stubbornness and aggressiveness, which Hemingway may have regarded as particularly Jewish characteristics and which were needed in a character who had to be in constant opposition to the others. And note that Cohn is far from a coward; he is even a bit of a bully and very handy with his fists, points usually approved by Hemingway. Also he is constant in his passion for Lady Brett. But none of this counts against his obtuseness, his failure to "get it," his inability to see the art in bull fighting, his unawareness of his own lack of charm, his unavailability to the lure of the great moments of life, in short, his lamentable lack of style.

The enormous popularity of Hemingway's novels and stories has often surprised me. It seems odd to me that so many should enjoy his descriptions of thrills available only to the very brave and the ultrasensitive and his derision of the satisfactions available to the multitude. But the answer may be that many readers like to fantasize themselves as heroes and some even to imagine that they are. Or is it simply that they admire a great writer and a great storyteller and do not bother to consider whether or not they would measure up to the author's standards? Indeed, why should they care?

Like Fitzgerald he brought a great art to a minor vision of life. Unless you are willing to see it as a great vision. Some, no doubt, do.

William Makepeace Thackeray

ILLIAM MAKEPEACE THACKERAY was the literary idol of the 1840s and 50s. The revered author of *Vanity Fair, Pendennis,* and *The Newcomes,* the avidly read contributor to *Punch,* the renowned wit and god of the Garrick Club, he had no rival in British letters but Charles Dickens. It may seem a little odd to readers of our day that he was once severely taken to task for his cynicism, for his disparagement of snobbery and toadyism in London society seems mild enough by our standards. If he deplored marrying for money and fawning upon the rich and nobly born, it hardly disguises from a modern eye his basic acceptance of the British class system and the Victorian moral code. His obvious love of the Britain of his own day, his admiration of the empire and the military, his bland acceptance of the subjugation of India, and his evident pleasure in describing the grandeur of even such a bad egg as Lord Steyne betrays that he is fencing with blunted foils. His heroines are chaste and pure, his heroes brave and virtuous, and his villains, like Barnes Newcome and Becky Sharp, receive condign punishment. The empire on which the sun never sets was perhaps intended by God to dominate the world.

All this, of course, is perfectly compatible with his being a great novelist, and however much his reputation may have declined in our day, *Vanity Fair* is still read as a major classic. It doesn't really matter that Thackeray violates all the rules laid down by Henry James for the writing of fiction. He introduces himself shamelessly into his stories, joking, moralizing, taking the reader into his confidence and brashly admitting that he's made the whole thing up. He skips in and out of the minds of his characters at will and even speculates on what may happen to them when their tale is finished. But on the whole he gets away with it. We are introduced, so to speak, into the artist's studio; we watch the painter at work and listen to the idle chatter with which he distracts himself and amuses us. We see his brushes, his oils, his unfinished canvases stacked against the walls, and we watch him at work. And then, little by little, we become aware of the great portrait that is being created before our very eyes, be it Becky Sharp or Major Pendennis or Colonel Newcome. Reading a Thackeray novel has a flavor all of its own; it can be a unique aesthetic experience.

But Thackeray was by no means always satisfied with the moral and aesthetic standards of his time. He admired the style and dignity and independent thinking of the eighteenth century, the so-called Age of Reason, which he thought contrasted favorably with the vulgar industrialization of the Victorian era. He was thoroughly grounded in its literature, and he became a scholar in his study of its politics and wars. Most of all, he envied its freedom from the prurient criticism of his own day. "Since the author of 'Tom Jones' was buried," he wrote once, "no writer of fiction has been permitted to depict to his utmost power a *Man*" (*English Humorists of the Eighteenth Century*).

Yet this nostalgia for an earlier day was drastically qualified by Thackeray's disgust at the moral looseness of the century of Fielding, Sterne, and Congreve, and this disgust was intensified by the passage of years. Ultimately he even turned on the author of *Tom Jones:*

> I can't say that I think Mr. Jones a virtuous character; I can't say but I think Fielding's evident liking and admiration of Mr. Jones shows that the great humorist's moral sense was blunted by his life, and that here in Art and Ethics, there is a great error.

And this is his judgment of Sterne:

> There is not a page in Sterne's writing but has something that were better away, a latent corruption—a hint as of an impure presence . . . I think of these past writers and of one who lives amongst us now, and am grateful for the innocent laughter and unsullied page which the author of "David Copperfield" gives to my children.

Even the sublime Congreve is not spared:

> All this pretty morality you have in the comedies of William Congreve, Esq. They are full of wit. Such manners as he observes, he observes with great humour; but ah! it's a weary feast, that banquet of wit where no love is. It palls very soon; sad indigestions follow it and lonely blank headaches in the morning.

Thackeray has returned at last to his own era.

It was, however, the period from the deposition of James II to the death of Queen Anne that he chose for the setting of his great novel *Esmond,* and he succeeded there in evoking the times with a vividness and an accuracy rare indeed in the danger-laden field of historical fiction. The story of the Castlewoods from their taking the king's side in the Glorious Revolution to their unsuccessful plot to seat the son of the exiled James on the throne of the dying Anne, narrated by Henry Esmond, a supposed family bastard, is both exciting and convincing. Oh, yes, there are a few too many military campaigns —to show off, perhaps, the depth of the author's conscientious research— but they are a brief part of the novel and easily skimmed over. The bulk of the tale is riveting, and Thackeray made a strong and deliberate effort to keep himself out of it. His other novels had been published in monthly install-ments, which encouraged disorganization, looseness and authorial asides, and he was determined that *Esmond* should be a tight and seamless work of art.

Which on the whole it is. Yet Thackeray is still with us in the personality of his hero. Henry Esmond is a kind of ambassador from the nineteenth cen-tury visiting the eighteenth, in some ways like Ralph Pendrel in Henry James's *The Sense of the Past,* who actually succeeds in translating himself from present-day London to the time of the Georges. Henry Esmond is as serious as the most serious Victorian, and he is moral to the point of being, so far as we can tell, a virgin to women in his middle thirties. Although he can cope with the times as an expert swordsman, an intrepid warrior, and a shrewd negotiator, and although he is admired by his fellow men, they see him as too sober, too moral—they call him "Parson Esmond," as if they instinctively sensed in him a different code of manners. But he provides Thackeray with a nineteenth-century eye with which to view—and to judge—the customs and practices of the eighteenth. If *Esmond* is the one novel in which he chose to suppress his "I," that is how he got around it.

Esmond's romance with Rachel Castlewood has something of a neuras-thenic quality. To me it smacks a good deal more of Thackeray's own day than of Fielding's or Congreve's. It *could* have happened in Queen Anne's day, of course; any kind of romance could have. Tom Jones, after all, fears for a while that the loose woman with whom he has spent the night may be his long lost mother. But it fits more smoothly into the Victorian epoch.

Rachel is depicted as the purest and most saintly of women, but Thack-eray endows her with one unpleasant characteristic: she is morbidly jealous, to the point of not allowing any even faintly good-looking women to be employed in the castle, to guard her philandering husband from temptation.

But despite her passionate loyalty to her spouse, his infidelity and ill treatment of her at last undermine her devotion to him, and she falls in love with the sixteen-year-old Harry Esmond, a household dependent then believed to be a family bastard. Poor Rachel suffers bitter pangs of remorse over this adulterous but hidden passion, and when her husband's death obliterates its sinfulness, it is only for her to discover that Harry has fallen in love with her beautiful but cold-hearted and worldly daughter, Beatrice. Yet she manages, heroically, to restrain her jealousy and to promote a match which she believes to be in the best interests of both. Harry has been revealed to her as a fine military officer and his base birth a lie. But Beatrice thinks she can do better, and when her treacherous conduct in the plot to restore the pretender destroys Harry's love for her, and he turns at last to her mother, Rachel and he marry and go off to a happy life in the new world. And this despite the difference in their ages and the quasi-mother-son relationship that has seemed until then to unite them.

The marriage of Harry and Lady Castlewood created considerable disgust among some of Thackeray's most devoted readers. It seemed to them to have an incestuous aroma. It has. But in our time, when we are much more conscious of the close ties of different kinds of love and of the role that sex plays in even the most seemingly Platonic friendships, we have no need to be disenchanted. We can accept the author's assurance that the Henry Esmonds' marriage was happily consummated and fruitful, for the twin brothers of *The Virginians* will be their grandchildren. We may even find it sexy that Rachel, the saint, should at last have her young man in bed. But I maintain that the deep seriousness with which Rachel and Harry take every step of their long and intimate relationship, her agony over her passion, and his long and persistent ignorance of it, have more to do with the dawn of Victorian morality than the ribaldry of the age of Fielding. Henry Esmond may be a kind of Joseph Andrews, but Fielding is laughing at Andrews and Thackeray is not for a minute laughing at Esmond. "Henry Esmond" could no more have been written by Fielding than "In Memoriam" by Alexander Pope.

Willa Cather and
Sinclair Lewis

N O WRITER'S WORK is more bathed in the author's personality than Willa Cather's. Her love of the expansive prairies of the American Southwest and her nostalgia for the simple farming life of the last decades of the nineteenth century permeate her finest chapters. Here is Jim Burden's boyhood introduction to the Nebraskan landscape in *My Antonia*:

> I can remember exactly how the country looked to me on that early September morning. Perhaps the glide of long railway travel was still with me, for more than anything else I felt motion in the landscape, in the fresh, easy-blowing morning wind, and in the earth itself, as if the shaggy grass were a sort of loose hide, and underneath herds of wild buffalo were galloping, galloping. . . .

It might be Cather herself describing her first girlhood vision of Nebraska when her family moved there from Virginia. It probably is. Indeed, the whole of *My Antonia* is very likely a personal reminiscence. It has no other discernible form. Jim Burden simply relates, one by one, in more or less chronological order, the principal impressions of his youth: the neighboring farmers and the stories of their earlier lives in Bohemia or Hungary, the killing of a giant rattlesnake, the local girls who leave the farms to earn money for their parents as servants in the nearest town, the murder committed by a vicious miser, and, finally, Jim's love for the hardy and resolute, but smiling, sunny-natured, and beautiful Antonia Shimerda, who is somehow the spirit of the whole wonderful countryside. We see everything through Burden's eyes or hear what he has heard.

Cather told her friend Elizabeth Sergeant that she wanted to show her heroine from all sides. She doesn't quite do this. We learn very little, for example, of Antonia's unhappy affair with a philanderer who deserts her and her bastard child. But it isn't that we need to know more. Antonia, as remembered by Jim Burden, is a sufficiently lovely picture. For the novel is not so much about Antonia as it is about someone's memory of Antonia; it is a book about nostalgia.

Cather once put her theory that an author's personality is his best material right on the line:

> If he tries to meddle with its vague outline, to twist it into some categorical shape, above all if he tries to adapt or modify its mood, he destroys its value. In working with this material he finds that he need have little to do with literary devices; he comes to depend more and more on something else—the thing by which our feet find the road home on a dark night, accounting of themselves for roots and stones which we had never noticed by day.

What unifies the novel, what covers up the seeming aimlessness of its construction, is the serene, golden mood of recaptured time created by Cather's seamless prose. It seems to Jim Burden that on the flat, endless Nebraska plains one could walk to the very edge of the earth:

> The light air about me told me that the world ended here: only the ground and sun and sky were left, and if one went a little farther there would be only sun and sky, and one would float off into them, like the tawny hawks which sailed over our heads making slow shadows on the grass."

Cather was by no means unaware of the crudities of American life: the money madness, the vulgarity, the low moral and artistic standards. But these were not her field. She once said that 1922 had broken the world in two and that she belonged to the earlier half. In a review of Montague Glass and Charles Klein's play *Potash and Perlmutter* she inveighed against the deterioration of city life in phrases that might have been written by Sinclair Lewis, whom she came greatly to admire: "This city roars and rumbles and hoots and jangles because Potash and Perlmutter are on their way to something."

Lewis was to pick up, so to speak, where she left off. He obtained a unique position in American letters as the author of *Main Street* and *Babbitt*, the chronicler of the pettiness, provincialism, and deadly boredom of middle-class urban life in the first half of the twentieth century. *Babbitt* has become a word in our language, and Lewis the spiritual partner of H. L. Mencken, to whom he dedicated *Elmer Gantry,* the darkest of his novels. Lewis was the great literary journalist of our fiction, for he explored a different aspect of American life in each of his books, including business, medicine, philanthropy, and religion, and he devoted months to intense research in each field that he proposed to treat.

One certainly cannot miss the saturnine quality of the author's personality in any of his books. The society that he depicts is steadily and remorselessly pummeled, and there is not much left of it when he is through. Yet in a curious way the reader's experience is rather exhilarating than depressing. I think that the reasons for this are threefold: first, that Lewis can be hilariously funny; one laughs rather than frowns. And second, that he is always fair. When he turns his gimlet eye on the European scene, for example, as he does in *Dodsworth,* he finds it equally ridiculous. Then, finally, he has a certain sympathy for even his silliest creations. They are, after all, human beings, and few are all bad. Elmer Gantry, who uses the ends of religion to further the vilest means, is a rare example of the irredeemable.

In *Main Street* we sympathize with Carol Kennicott's desperate efforts to instill a little culture and imagination into the arid society of Gopher Prairie, despite the fact that she is a bit of an ass and fails fully to appreciate the good work and fine character of the hard-working country doctor she has married. We pity her plight even as we recognize how foolishly she is trying to remedy it. But it is in *Babbitt* that we sense the full stretch of Lewis's basic tolerance and understanding.

George F. Babbitt, despite the pressure of all his friends, family, and business associates, with whom until then he has been totally congenial, and at risk to his successful real estate business, finally summons up the courage to defend the strikers in a labor dispute that has torn the town of Zenith in two. And he compounds this heresy by turning down an invitation to join the much-coveted (at least in his set) Good Citizens' League, a right-wing organization that he feels is hostile to basic civil liberties.

In the end he gives in and joins the league. His wife has survived a dangerous operation, and the warm congratulations of his old friends, plus his relief that she has not died and added to his guilt at having treated her unkindly, make him realize how lonely, bereft, and perhaps actually impoverished he will be if he continues in his independent stance. Lewis very aptly makes us feel Babbitt's inner glow at being taken back into the clan in which he has known the only happy moments of his life. It doesn't matter that the clan is repulsive to the reader. Babbitt is rejoining the only world that could care about him; one doubts his capacity to find another, or to endure the loss of his old consolations. What he has done, even at the price he has to pay, is probably all that we can or should expect of the poor guy. We sense his relief at the Boosters' Club lunch where he is at last again welcome: "He knew by the cheer that he was secure again and popular; he knew that he would no more endanger his security and popularity by straying from the Clan of Good Fellows."

John P. Marquand

A CENTRAL THEME of the old novel of manners is snobbishness. Sometimes the snobbishness is religious, sometimes intellectual, sometimes even athletic, but for the most part it is simply social: the ancient disdain of an upper class for a lower. It is in the absurdity and cruelty of such attitudes that Jane Austen and Thackeray and Trollope and Balzac and Proust joyfully feasted. Their snobs might be comic, like Lady Catherine de Bourgh, or vicious, like Barnes Newcome, or pathetic like the Baron de Charlus, or even redeemable, like Fitzwilliams Darcy, but they are always there, and playing major parts in the story. Trollope indeed crossed the line into the ridiculous in *Marion Fay,* in which his hero, a postal clerk, is made eligible to marry the daughter of a marquis by the last-minute discovery that he is actually the unacknowledged son of an Italian duke!

One might have thought that the drastic democratization of the English-speaking world in the last hundred years would have reduced the demand for this one-time staple of the novelist of manners, but it seems to have been possessed of an enduring quality. If the once-haughty have learned to curb or at least conceal their illusion of innate superiority, their potential victims have shown a remorseless memory. The day when a Voltaire could be beaten up by a nobleman's lackeys may be happily past, but the merest hint of a lifted eyebrow can still engender a mortal hate. Our communications, both private and public, oral or printed, are now pruned of words that might offend the tenderest of feelings in matters of race, ethnical origin, religion, or sexual preference. In a recent film version of *Showboat* the word *niggers* was omitted from the song "Old Man River" though Paul Robeson had used it with sobering and powerful significance in the original production.

The subject of social snobbishness is a keynote in the novels of John P. Marquand, and its validity as a principal topic can be gauged by the era in which each of his novels is set. It should not be surprising that its validity increases as the author moves into the past. Marquand was born to a family of old and revered colonial stock; for generations they had been prominent citizens of Newburyport, Massachusetts, just north of Boston. But while he was still a boy, his father ineptly lost his money, and young John was removed from a private to a public school, with the result that when he went to Harvard (on money desperately scraped together) he didn't know the social leaders of the class, all privately educated, and didn't make a "proper" club. He was to make all the "right" connections later in life and even marry a Boston Sedgwick, but he would always remember the days when he was on the other side of the fence, and he cherished a lifelong sense of what it was like to be disdained by persons who had simply enjoyed a more privileged upbringing. This was to prove the chief asset and the ultimate flaw in his remarkable literary talent.

In *The Late George Apley* he used his intimate knowledge of the prejudices and inhibitions of Old Boston society to brilliant advantage and produced a near classic in American letters. His memory of old snubs, somewhat softened by his later inclusion in that snubbing world, enabled him to portray his protagonist and the Apley family not only with rich humor but with a definite compassion as well. It is comedy in the highest and most serious vein, worthy of George Meredith in *The Egoist*. It is funny; it is sad, and it is true. George Apley is as noble-minded as he is ridiculous. He is a kind of puritan Don Quixote, tilting at the windmills of a steadily encroaching modernism.

The pressures felt by Apley, born as he was in 1866 on the "steep part" of Mount Vernon Street on Beacon Hill, of Boston Brahmin parents, are indeed heavy enough to bind all but the most independent of souls. The probably ruthless origin of the family fortune in textile mills has been sufficiently buried in the past so that the high ethical standards now guiding the family could seem untainted to the young heir apparent. It is true that his old Uncle Will, now in charge of the business, is not averse to using the old tactics, but he sees that young George is not a man for the rough and tough of the marketplace and approves of his being confined to the investment of the family trusts and the management of the family charities. The result is that wherever George looks he sees only a seemingly solid respectability and a sober prosperity. Why indeed should anything be changed? Is it not his plain duty to pass on the good estate that he has inherited?

The novel is the story of his futile efforts to make some sort of a life of his own, as opposed to the life he has been given. For he is haunted by his sense that, however commendable may seem the code of the Apleys, it may not be the whole answer to the conundrum of his existence. He falls in love with and wants to marry an Irish Catholic girl, but he quails before the horror of the bristlingly united Apley clan who view the emigrants from Eire as the old Romans did the Goths. How could he subject his beloved to the reception such a bride would get? He accepts his fate and marries a seemingly meek and proper Boston girl who collects old butter knives and rapidly evolves into the most husband-dominating of matriarchs. He buys a camp in the Maine woods to find occasional escape from the stultifying sameness of his urban social life, but his wife follows him and brings with her all that he has tried to flee. He wants to understand his children but by the time they are grown he has already been atrophied to a point where he cannot fathom their new values. The cleverest part of the novel is in the quotations from his letters and public addresses, in which one follows the gradual desiccation of his soul and the ultimate triumph of moral platitudes over heartfelt ideals— all against the gloomy backdrop of his own half-awareness of what is really going on. With each step he has made towards liberation another rope has been flung around his neck.

The story is told by an old friend and contemporary of Apley's, who is writing, after the latter's death in 1933, what he had planned to be the traditionally laudatory, privately printed memoir for the decedent's acquaintances, but in which he is having to include, at the insistence of Apley's son and daughter, material of a much more revealing nature. The fact that the memoirist, very much an Apley type himself, would never have agreed to insert some of this material, and would have quit his job rather than do so, need not concern us too much. How else are we to learn the truth about Apley? It is a flaw that the reader only notices when he has finished reading the novel.

H. M. Pulham, Esquire might almost be about a son of George Apley, although the father of the eponymous hero is represented as belonging to the nouveau riche. The family, however, have managed to become accepted by Boston's upper crust, and the protagonist of the novel, born in Brookline in 1892, has been sent to the right boarding school, St. Swithin's, and at Harvard has joined the right crowd and made the right club. He is already nestled in the groove where it is expected that he will spend a contented lifetime when World War I intervenes. At the front he unexpectedly proves himself an undoubted hero and is awarded the Distinguished Service Medal. Stopping in New York on his way home after the armistice, he finds himself caught up in a mood of novel independence, engendered by the violence of battle, and he allows himself to be persuaded by Bill King, the sole liberal friend he made at Harvard, to stay in Manhattan and work for an advertising agency instead of returning to Boston to sell bonds.

Pulham not only has the guts to defy his shocked parents and make a go of this new business; he falls in love with and proposes to marry Marvin Miles, a smart young woman with no social credentials but who is well on her way to the top as an advertiser and who fully returns his devotion. Unfortunately Pulham's father picks this moment to die, and Pulham has to return to Boston to look after his mother and attend to saving what he can of the much depleted family fortune. Faced with his decision that it is his unavoidable duty to live permanently in Boston and assume what he regards as his inherited obligations, Marvin Miles gives him up. She declines to be smothered in the life that he feels he must lead, and, however agonized, Pulham accepts her decision.

And then, of course, he is lost. He enters into a tepid marriage with an old girlfriend and takes up a tepid career as an investment counselor in the bond firm that employed him before the war. His old college crowd provides him with friendship, and his two children are mildly companionable. His life flows along in a moderately pleasant fashion without much challenge or excitement and will presumably continue to do so after the book ends. He doesn't even know that his wife has had an affair with his friend Bill King. But she will never leave him. King no more wants to marry her than Marvin wanted to marry Pulham. King knows that the Pulhams are two of a kind.

As the book is cast in the form of Pulham's autobiography, the reader must glean the wife's affair through what Pulman lets drop. But the fact that he fails to deduce what the reader can't help but deduce makes him appear considerably stupider than Marquand intended him to be. But this, unlike the narrative quirk mentioned in the discussion of *The Late George Apley,* hurts the novel by making the hero something of an ass, at least in that chapter.

Where *Pulman* fails and *Apley* succeeds is in Marquand's failure to see the radical drop in the effective power of social prejudices in the time that elapsed between the birth dates of the two protagonists. Apley is doomed; Pulham dooms himself. By the 1920s there simply was not enough force left in the Old Boston traditions to keep a man of any strength of character—let alone a war hero—from choosing to live in New York if that was required—and reasonably required, for was he not already happily living there?—by the girl he passionately adores. Pulham is weak, and weaker than the man Marquand seems to have had in mind. Boston would have soon enough come to accept

Pulham the New Yorker, nor would it have taken long for his family and friends to appreciate a woman as charming as Marvin Miles.

Marquand himself practically admits this when he has Pulham describe Bill King's career at Harvard:

> Bill would have actually got on very well at Harvard, I think if he had cared about trying. It was true that he did not have any connections, but if he had gone out for something else besides the Dramatic Club, such as the Lampoon, or even the Crimson, and if he had bothered with the people to whom I had introduced him and who usually liked him, he would very possibly have made a Club.

If a writer is going to base a novel on social barriers today, he had better seek areas where they still exist in all their rigor. Asia is still full of them.

E. M. Forster

E M. FORSTER put more of himself into his fiction than any other great English novelist since Thackeray. He never hesitated to insert what was frankly his own personal point of view. Thus he says of Mrs. Bast in *Howards End:* "Poor Jackie! She was not a bad sort and had a great deal to bear." On the other hand "poor Mrs. Charles" in the same novel "is a rubbishy little creature, and she knew it." And he speculates: "Ought the Wilcoxes to have offered their home to Margaret? I think not." Nor does he scruple to submit his reader to his own personal and highly individual theories on any social issues raised by some twist in his plot. "Actual life is full of false clues and sign-posts that lead nowhere. The most successful career must show a waste of strength that might have moved mountains, and the most unsuccessful is not that of the man who is taken unprepared, but of him who is prepared but never taken."

He carries this freedom into the field of literary method. In the tangled question of from what point or points of view the action of a story should be seen, he rejects entirely the strict rules laid down by Henry James, that self-appointed cleaner-up of the messy Victorian novel. James confines his reader either to a single point of view for a whole book, such as Strether's in *The Ambassadors,* or to a succession of points of view, each operating alone in the section of the novel assigned to it. Forster, having astutely pointed out in his *Aspects of the Novel* that such distinctions were of greater importance to the writer than to the reader, happily allowed himself to jump in and out of the minds of his characters at will, as he unfolded his tale.

Nor does he hesitate to kill off a character right after introducing him with a careful description that leads the reader to expect that such a one will play a major part in the story. "Gerald died that afternoon. He was broken up in the football match." And he will guide his reader firmly away from questions which do not bear on the issues he seeks to present. "We are not concerned with the very poor. They are unthinkable and only to be approached by the statistician or the poet" (*Howards End*).

One should not infer from this, however, that Forster was not a careful craftsman. He allowed himself what he regarded as a necessary freedom to illustrate the diverse and bizarre philosophies and habits of the British upper-middle class in the early years of the twentieth century, and how much such ideas and habits inhibited their enjoyment of the fuller life. It was not that he regarded his own countrymen as particularly deficient in this respect (though one may at moments suspect this); it is more that he considered their illusions common to the "modern world," and that he found his fellow Englishmen what he had nearest to hand.

For so large a field Forster could not limit himself to a single sentient observer, like James's Strether. The nearest he would come to this was Margaret Schlegel in *Howards End* and Fielding in *A Passage to India*. But for most of his fiction he needed multiple points of view, including his own, and much of the same illogic in the sequence of events that we find in life. For what he was attempting to illustrate—to reduce it to simplest terms—was what happened to animal man when he put on clothes to cover his nakedness.

These clothes to Forster were all the little dos and don'ts, the petty prejudices and snobberies, the silly sentimentalities and religious hypocrisies that make up the veneer of what so many of his contemporaries considered civilization. As Forster saw it, these little things blinded people to the values of the good life. They were distractions that stood between mankind and the liberty of spirit which is one essential to any real happiness. And they blocked human communication, the basis of mutual understanding, which is the other. "Only connect" was Forster's famed motto. While we are chained to shibboleths, we are still children. We are not serious; we play with life.

The British tourists in Italy provided Forster with a subject peculiarly appropriate to his satirical pen. He saw them as more comic than ominous, more naive than ill-natured, and the reaction to them of the more natural, simpler, and much more direct denizens of Florence and Rome brings out vividly the yawning gulf between two cultures. When Forster in *A Passage to India* turns his satirical genius to the depiction of what happens when the British, with all their hang-ups, are seen as conquerors and no longer as innocent tourists, he reaches not only tragedy but greatness.

His second most important novel, *Howards End,* however, deals with England alone and the conflict between two radically different philosophies arising within the United Kingdom. On one side are the Schlegel sisters,

Margaret and Helen, representing the life of the intellect and of the spirit, inspired by the arts and deeply concerned with the unfortunates of the earth. On the other are the "useful people," the Wilcoxes, Henry, the magnate, and his children, standing for the forces that supposedly keep the machinery of everyday life turning. Henry is a fond parent and an efficient man of affairs; he takes immediate control of everybody and everything, including Margaret Schlegel, whom he marries. He is not a bad man—Forster hardly believes in bad men—but he has little heart for those who are crushed in competing businesses. The conflict between the Schlegels and Wilcoxes is brought to a head by the fate of a poor clerk, Leonard Bast, a protégé of Helen's, who is ruined by a business tip casually offered by Henry, a wrong compounded by the discovery that Mrs. Bast had been seduced by Henry years before. A complicated plot ends when Bast is killed by Henry's son. The wretched clerk, like Rosencrantz and Guildenstern in *Hamlet,* is the baser nature who has fallen "between the pass and fell incensed points of mighty opposites."

Fourteen years and a world war intervened between the publication of *Howards End* (1910) and *A Passage to India* (1924). Forster's first four novels are brilliant satires, but he had yet to show what he could do with a subject of greater, of international importance. He had observed India and the Raj at first hand; he had a keen idea of the things that were basically and hopelessly wrong with the imperial system. And to demonstrate what these were he didn't need his old tool of satire. Realism could be counted on to serve instead. For we are no longer facing the essentially comic aspect of the misunderstanding between two nationalities, as with British and Italians; we are brought up against the tragic results of such a difference when one race is the conqueror of another. Not that there aren't comic situations in *A Passage to India;* it wouldn't a Forster creation without them. But the central message of the book is a grim one: the British occupation of India corrupts both the ruled and the rulers and had better not continue.

Is it then a work of propaganda, like *Uncle Tom's Cabin?* Although every incident of harshness to slaves in Harriet Beecher Stowe's classic is based on a fact, the episodes are strung together in such a way as to convey an unduly cruel picture of life in the Old South. Stowe did this on purpose to show what *could* happen under such a system. But Forster did not need to touch up his picture. He didn't have to show a single instance of injustice. All he had to do was produce one episode: an English woman's mistaken claim that an Indian had assaulted her, to bring out in the open all the suspicion, resentment, and prejudice of both races. The accusation is withdrawn, and the status quo restored, but the curtain has been drawn aside, and we have glimpsed the essential vulnerability of British imperialism.

Forster may have tried to be fair to both sides, but his sympathies are all with the Indians. He shows the latter, largely through his vivid depiction of the young doctor, Aziz, as bright, charming, agreeable, and possessed of good, if too artificially formal, manners, but at the same time touchy, overly sensitive, too quick to see a mortal rebuff in the least appearance of coolness. And Forster also makes it clear that the Indians are the victims of superstition and prone to dangerous religious intolerance among themselves.

The British, of course are seen less favorably. Indeed, most of them are quite terrible in their smug superiority and snooty treatment of the natives. One illustration may suffice. Their cherished club, where no natives are usually allowed, even as guests, is opened to the Indians on a rare occasion in the interest of better racial relations. The party is hardly a success.

> The Englishmen had intended to play up better, but had been prevented from doing so by their women folk, whom they had to attend, provide with tea, advise about dogs, etc. When tennis began, the barrier grew impenetrable. It had been hoped to have some sets between East and West, but this was forgotten, and the courts were monopolized by the usual club couples.

Even when an Englishman arrives in the colony as a fairly decent fellow, he soon changes. Adela Quested notes this change in Ronny Heaslop, whom she has come to India to marry:

> India had developed sides of his character that she had never admired. His self-complacency, his censoriousness, his lack of subtlety, all grew vivid beneath a tropic sky; he seemed more indifferent than of old to what was passing in the minds of his fellows, more certain that he was right about them, or that if he was wrong it didn't matter. When proved wrong, he was particularly exasperating; he always managed to suggest that she needn't have bothered to prove it. The point she made was never the relevant point, her arguments conclusive but barren, she was reminded that he had expert knowledge, and she none, and that experience would not help her because she could not interpret it. A Public School, London University, a year at a crammer's, a particular series of posts in a particular province, a fall from a horse and a touch of fever were presented to her as the only training by which Indians and all who reside in their country can be understood.

Cyril Fielding, principal of the local college for Indian students, is the only Englishman in the colony who has any real understanding of or sympathy for the Indians. Of course, he has the advantage over the others that he was over forty when he came to India and had a character already formed and the courage to take an unpopular stand in the matter of the falsely accused Aziz. In character, if not in appearance, he may have something in common with his creator.

> He was not unpatriotic; he always got on with Englishmen in England, all his best friends were English, so why was it not the same out here? Outwardly of the large shaggy type, with sprawling limbs and blue eyes, he appeared to inspire confidence until he spoke. Then something in his manner puzzled people and failed to allay the distrust which his profession naturally inspired. There needs must be this evil of brains in India, but woe to him by whom they are increased! The feeling grew that Mr. Fielding was a disruptive force, and rightly, for ideas are fatal to caste, and he used ideas by that most potent method—interchange.

Fielding is essentially, like the author, an observer of the action in the novel; he does not affect its outcome except in his friendship with Aziz and his stalwart defense of the latter, after the mistaken accusation by Adela Quested, in the teeth of the British community. But Fielding's subsequent marriage in England to Adela's half-sister, Stella Moore, antagonizes Aziz, who is wrongly informed that he has married Adela, and the two men are not reconciled until the end of the book. Yet even then the reconcilement is not complete; India will always come between them.

The stupid misunderstandings have been cleared up, but socially they have no meeting place. Fielding has "thrown in his lot with Anglo-India by marrying a country woman, and he was acquiring some of its limitations, and already felt surprise at his own past heroism. Would he today defy his own people for the sake of a stray Indian?" And Aziz sees that they must part. In a fit of patriotism he wants to be rid of both Fielding and England, and he exclaims with what to Forster in 1924 was a rare clairvoyance: "Clear out, clear out, I say. Why are we put to so much suffering? We used to blame you, now we blame ourselves, we grow wiser. Until England is in difficulties we keep silent, but in the next European war—aha, aha! Then is our time."

What is never explained in the novel is the unexplainable: the significance of the echo that Mrs. Moore, Fielding's future mother-in-law, hears in the Marabar Caves, which has such a lasting and deeply depressing effect on her.

She, and her young son Ralph, who appears only at the very end of the novel, are represented as the only English persons with a spiritual affinity for the Orient, so the echo must have had something to do with the soul of India.

> What had spoken to her in that scoured out cavity in the granite? What dwelt in the first of the caves? Something very old and very small. Before time, it was, before space also. Something snub-nosed, incapable of generosity—the undying worm itself. Since hearing its voice, she had not entertained one large thought. . . . Visions are supposed to entail profundity, but—Wait till you get one, dear Reader!

And that is where Forster leaves us. We simply learn that Mrs. Moore died on the ship returning her to England.

Anatole France

ANATOLE FRANCE, whose eighty years of life spanned the War of 1870, the Commune, and World War I, who had passionately taken up the cause of Dreyfus and been a leader of radical political thought, who had been both a profound scholar and a literary luminary, had of course been the witness of much that was sordid and disheartening in the world around him, nor had he hesitated to address it in his many works. But the significant thing about him is that he never lost faith in the use of language to redeem the ugly. The beautiful and mellifluous prose in which he clad the restrained pessimism of his philosophy of life gives an enchanting unity to his voluminous work, be it fiction, criticism, history, or simply the belles lettres of his widely ranging thoughts and ideas. Indeed, one is not always quite sure in which category to place the volume one is reading. But one is always sure that it is by France.

He has fallen from the eminence critics once accorded him, but he is still widely appreciated, and I suspect will continue to be. Perhaps the personality that he so richly spreads over his work is most closely caught in the character of Brotteaux in *Les Dieux ont soif,* his great tale of the French Revolution. Brotteaux is a former aristocrat, now impoverished, who ekes out a humble living in a garret where he makes puppets for children. A convinced and cheerful atheist, he is stoically content with his pleasant memories of the fuller life he has had the wit and good luck once to lead, and with his devotion to classical literature. When the Terror at last catches up with him, and he is about to be sent to the guillotine, together with the devout old priest with whom he has generously shared his attic, he is reading Lucretius.

A l'arrivée de l'executeur et de ses valets, Brotteaux, qui lisait tranquillement son Lucrèce, mit le signet à la page commencée, ferma le livre, le fourra dans la poche de sa redingote et dit a sa barnabite:

—Mon reverend Père, ce dont j'enrage, c'est que je ne vous persuaderai pas. Nous allons dormir tous deux notre dernier sommeil, et je ne pourrai pas vous tirer par la manche et vous reveiller pour vous dire: "Vous voyez vous n'avez ni sentiment ni connaissance; vous êtes inanime. Ce qui suit la vie est comme ce qui la précède."

Il voulût sourire; mais une atroce douleur lui saisit le coeur et les entrailles et il fût près de défaillir.

Il reprit toutefois:

—Mon Père, je vous laisse voir ma faiblesse. J'aime la vie et ne la quitte point sans regret.

The French Revolution has, of course, provided a rich source of plots for a multitude of novels, but no writer has made a more vivid and valid use of it than France in *Les Dieux ont soif.* He had studied the revolution in depth from his earliest years; his father had kept a bookshop in Paris devoted entirely to literature on the subject. France's protagonist, Evariste Gamelin, a flamingly radical youth, romantically pale-faced with long black hair, has a blind and passionate faith in the Revolution and is eager to hunt down and punish any who may be aiding the foreign powers that are invading France for the purpose of restoring the monarchy. Appointed a juror on a court designed to try traitors, he adopts the Jacobin principle that a man is presumed guilty until proven innocent, and he jubilantly sends people, including his own brother-in-law, to the guillotine on the slightest suspicion of the mildest disloyalty to the republic. Yet this is also the man who, in starving, war-torn Paris, will give his precious ration of bread to a hungry woman standing in the line behind him, who is chaste to the point of hardly daring to kiss the woman he loves, and who tenderly supports his old mother and looks after her every want.

The novel dramatically equates the frenzied acceleration of killing in the Terror with Gamelin's waxing lust for traitors' blood until a kind of mass hysteria grips Paris, and victims seem as anxious to receive the fatal blow as the accusers are to accord it. When the Revolution, which has now turned against its own children, at last culminates in the execution of Robespierre and his gang, and Gamelin, faithful to the bitter end to the "sea-green incorruptible," finds himself condemned to death, his last reflections in the cart bearing him to the fatal knife are that he had deserved his fate for being too lenient on the enemies of liberty.

Je meurs justement. Il est juste que nous recevons ces outrages jetés a la République et dont nous aurions dû la défendre. Nous avons été faibles; nous nous sommes rendus coupables d'indulgence. Nous avons trahi la République. Nous avons merité notre sort. Robespierre lui-même, le pur, le saint, a peché par douceur, par mansuétude; ses fautes sont effacées par son martyr. A son exemple j'ai trahi la République; elle périt: il est juste que je meure avec elle.

France understood that his Gamelin was the bastard child of the romantic movement inaugurated by Rousseau, of the *comédie larmoyante,* of the eighteenth-century idolization of the natural man, the savage. Uncontrolled sentimentality had spawned sadism. The Byronic hero had become a real corsair: a monster. Gamelin was very likely modeled on Saint-Just, Robespierre's handsome and remorseless right-hand man. He is an unforgettable character.

As in all his novels, France never hesitates to interrupt the flow of his story by inserting a discussion among his characters that may have little to do with the furthering of his plot, but which brings up topics of general interest to both author and reader. The remarkable thing about these is that they are always interesting and somehow manage to fit into the atmosphere of the story. Brotteaux's sardonic discussions with Gamelin about the proper function of government, and his arguments with the old priest about religion, are amusing in themselves, without regard to the horror of the revolution tightening around them. For France himself, like his character Brotteaux, seems always to preserve his detachment, even before the knife of the guillotine; he weaves his tale in beautiful sentences as if he were reminding us that the world has always been full of horrible things and that the best we can do is to make a work of art out of our account of them.

In *Le Lys Rouge,* perhaps his finest novel, France draws a much quieter scene. Thérèse Martin, a great heiress and a great beauty, married childlessly and lovelessly to a future cabinet minister who is perfectly willing to tolerate any lover of hers so long as she gives him the money he needs and acts as his hostess, finds herself bored with society, with her faithful lover Menil, and with her existence in general. She has no real challenge in life, and she escapes to Florence to visit a friend there, an English poetess, and seek distraction in a beautiful Italian spring. There the unexpected happens to her, for she falls in love, very deeply and for the first time, with a French sculptor, Dechartre, and he with her. They find brief but ecstatic happiness in a torrid love affair, but when he discovers that she has been Menil's lover just before their meeting he suffers an attack of jealousy so agonizing that he leaves her forever. That is all that happens, but the felt beauty of the heroine and the intensity and misery of her love, projected against the glorious background of Florence, give France the supreme opportunity to bathe us in his peerless prose.

Here he has, with the poetess and her guests, multiple occasions for discussions of art, politics, history, and philosophy that we listen to with an interest that seems oddly enhanced by our simultaneous realization that the heroine is listening and occasionally briefly joining in with only half a mind, the other half being intent on the next rendezvous with her lover.

But I have a perhaps too personal a reaction. Dechartre's fatal jealousy is bothersome to me. Do I feel that France, like Proust, is taking an absurdly excessive emotion too seriously? Is it a French upper-class exaggeration of a natural but not-impossible-to-moderate desire to *own* a woman? The product of an idle society where the men have little to do but hunt animals and make love to women? And I wrong to cross Dechartre off as an ass?

Renan in his *Vie de Jésus* wrote, "Dans sa retraite, Pilate ne songea probablement pas un moment à l'episode oublié qui devait transmettre sa triste renommée à la posterité las plus lointaine." In this sentence France found the source of his story "Le Procurateur de Judée," in which Aelius Lamia, an old Roman of the noble class, visiting the baths of Baies near Pompei, runs into the litter of his old friend Pontius Pilate, the retired Procurator of Judea, and is invited to dine with him at his villa. There they discuss the old times in Jerusalem, where they first met, in the course of which Lamia asks his host if by any chance he remembers a thaumaturge, later crucified, whose group a Jewish dancing girl that Lamia admired had quit her profession to follow. His name was Jesus. Pilate shakes his head. "Jésus? Je ne me rappelle pas." Not until Edith Wharton ended "Roman Fever" with the "I had Barbara" has a short story ended with so dramatically effective a last line.

The Pilate story is France at his very best. He loved to write of classic times, which his style effectively evoked. Like his favorite poet Racine, he adapted himself with grace and ease to the legends of ancient Greece and Rome.

George Meredith

AT THE TIME of George Meredith's death in 1909, his literary reputation was at its zenith. There were critics, even some of the best, who did not hesitate to rate him one of the greatest British novelists, the equal if not the superior to Dickens, Thackeray, and Eliot, and he had become a cult figure with the young intellectuals of Oxford and Cambridge. But since then his popularity and critical standing have steadily dropped until today, when *The Egoist* stands almost alone of his novels to be recommended reading in college English courses.

As I attribute much of this decline to the profusion of his personality throughout his fiction, it seems appropriate to end this volume with an extensive survey of his life and work with particular emphasis on their intimate relationship.

Meredith himself is always present to his readers. He is sitting, so to speak, before us, and chatting at considerable length—interruption is not to be thought of—about the vicissitudes of his characters, commenting freely and frankly on their oddities and the problems with his devious plots, expressing his views on politics, military preparedness, and the corrupting vulgarity of a money-mad society, picking up his neglected tale and dropping it again at will to give vent to his constant editorializing. He takes sides almost violently for or against a particular character, often when he seems to suspect the reader of disagreeing with him. And he is not only the novelist and philosopher; he is also the poet, and his lyrical descriptions of the rural countryside seem more for the reader's delectation than for the setting of mood to accord with the action. If the reader happens to like this, he is hooked, but I suspect that a modern one finds it detrimental to the unfolding of the story and will slam the book shut.

Meredith in life was notoriously supposed to be reticent about his background and personal history. Perhaps that is why fiction was his needed outlet.

Considerable emphasis has been placed by biographers of George Meredith on the fact that both his grandfather and father were tailors, and that he was always known to be reticent in discussing his family background. Unfortunately for Meredith, if concealment of a social disability was actually his purpose, his grandfather Melchisidec Meredith, a naval tailor in Portsmouth, was a legend in his lifetime, an ebullient character who behaved more like a marquis than a "snip," who befriended admirals and rode heartily to hounds. Furthermore, as if to compound the disability, Meredith put his famous grandfather into an early novel, *Evan Harrington,* gave him the name Melchisidec, and endowed him with three snobbish daughters who spent their lives disavowing the relationship, as had indeed in life Meredith's three aunts. It has puzzled his chroniclers that he should have so blatantly exposed what at all other times he seemed so anxious to conceal. But of course he had always to be aware that the facts of his background were available to anyone willing to take the trouble to track them down.

J. B. Priestly concocted the interesting theory that Meredith was not so much ashamed of the tailors in his family as of the fact that in his youth he *had* been ashamed of them. And one must remember that class consciousness has always been a salient feature in British social life and that in Meredith's day it was peculiarly rife. Henry James made the point that his social success in the highest strata of London life was much facilitated by the fact that, as an American, he belonged to no identifiable class.

Perhaps Siegfried Sassoon, always a man of shrewd sense, put it best in his biography of Meredith:

> My explanation, therefore, amounts to no more than this: that once the creator in him was active, the personal dilemma of his origin was transformed into a grand opportunity for a serio-comic extravaganza. Let it also be conceded that while writing the book [*Evan Harrington*] he worked out of his system the lurking resentment he had felt at not having been born a gentleman. Naturally, he had found it a nuisance to be the "son of a snip." But he was now taking advantage of that situation and doing it with relish.

Meredith was born in Portsmouth in 1828, of Augustus Meredith, who succeeded to his late father's tailoring business there, and his wife, the former Jane Macnamara, who died when her son and only child was five. Meredith always made much of his supposed Welsh ancestry—he endowed the Welsh with greater imagination than other Britons—but it seems that his forebears were largely English. Augustus Meredith was a financial bungler; he made a failure of the family business and moved to London and then to South Africa, and, to young George's distaste, he married his housekeeper. He drifted almost altogether out of the life of a son who subsisted entirely on a small inheritance from his mother and essentially brought himself up. After two years in the Moravian School at Neuweid on the Rhine, near Cologne, which he much enjoyed and whose liberal religious education spared him from insular prejudices, he returned to England to be apprenticed for a short term to a solicitor in London in whose chambers he read little law and wrote much poetry. He had no intention of being a lawyer.

At age twenty-one he married a beautiful and intellectual widow, Mary Nicholls, some half dozen years older than he and a daughter of Thomas Love Peacock, the novelist and friend of Shelley, and he attempted to support his new ménage by his writing. The attempt was not successful, nor was the couple happily mated. After nine years of wedlock Mary Meredith abandoned her husband and son Arthur and absconded to Capri with a lover, returning to England a year later with a baby born of her liaison. Meredith refused to take her back or even to let her see her son in the few years she had left before a premature demise. Some of his heartache was exposed in his long poem, "Modern Love," in which, however, despite his rigorous treatment of her in life, he divides the blame between the unfaithful wife and her spouse.

In 1866, at age 36, the widower Meredith was remarried, this time happily, to Mary Villiani, an amiable and lovable young woman of French descent, by whom he had two children, a son and daughter. Unfortunately, his older son Arthur, accustomed to the total devotion of a single parent, resented having to share that love with a stepmother and half-siblings, and this growing rift resulted at last in a near total estrangement between father and son. Meredith's other two children, however, were always entirely devoted to him, and their love helped to sustain him in his deep grief over the loss of his wife from cancer in 1885. For the remaining quarter century of his life he remained a widower, living alone in his cottage, Box Hill, in the beautiful Surrey countryside near Dorking, where notables of the literary and political worlds came to visit him.

For fame in the last decades of his life had at last come to him. He had from the beginning achieved considerable praise from critics—the great George Eliot had hailed his first novel—but many readers had found him difficult and obscure, and popularity had had to await publication of *Diana of the Crossways* and *The Egoist*. He had long supplemented his often inadequate writing income with occasional journalism and, later, as a reader and editor for

Chapman & Hall, where he had the distinction of being an early adviser to the young Thomas Hardy and the less-coveted one of having rejected Mrs. Henry Woods's later super best-seller *East Lynne.* He had become a legend in his lifetime.

Meredith, before the crippling illness of his last years, when he could no longer walk, was a splendid figure of a man, tall, muscular, red-headed, hearty and handsome, who loved to climb mountains in Switzerland and take long hikes in the Surrey downs. He was known as a genial host and a great talker, famed for his wit and joviality. This aspect of him—and a true one for so much of his long life—should be remembered in view of the fact that the fame that accompanied his closing years has left us with too many pictures of a sad, if rather beautiful, deaf old man in a wheelchair, with snowy white hair and beard.

The great esteem in which Meredith's work was held in his lifetime has not survived into our times. The obscurity of some of his prose, the oddness and seeming illogic of some of his plots, his loose habit of authorial digression, the didacticism of some of his preaching, all emphasized by many of his early critics, are echoed by later ones of today. *Diana of the Crossways, The Egoist,* and perhaps *The Ordeal of Richard Feverel* alone survive among modern readers, and even their tenure may be precarious. Yet almost every critic will admit that there is greatness to be found in Meredith, if one can only find it. And all admit that his fiction is unique.

Perhaps most important, he is always a poet, even in his novels. All agree that his descriptions of natural scenery are peerless. Banalities and bromides are not to be found in his work. His vision of life springs from deep insight and a distrust of ordinary observations and generally accepted classifications. He suspects the taken-for-granted logic of so much literary plotting. In the tangle of the seemingly inexplicable he seeks to unravel the soul. As J. B. Priestly has said in his *George Meredith:* "What he wishes to do is not to present us with an arresting and interesting chronicle of events, but to move from one scene to another as quickly and easily as possible." And Oscar Wilde adds to this: "His people not merely live, but they live in thought. . . . They are interpretive and symbolic." And Meredith himself sums it up: "Narrative is nothing. It is the mere vehicle of philosophy. The interest is in the idea which action serves to illustrate" (*Letters of George Meredith*).

I think we can see Meredith trying to spell out this concept in a letter written in 1888:

I have written always with the perception that there is no life but of the spirit; that the concrete is really the shadowy, yet that the way to the spiritual life lies in the complete unfolding of the creature, not in the nipping of his passions.

A letter of 1884 warns of the danger of following the blood rather than the spirit:

I would not have my life again—under the conditions—and also I should think it a vileness to crave for the happiest of renewed existences. The soul's one road is forward. Dreams of sensational desires drown it. But as to the soul we get the conception of that by contrast with the sensations. We go on and are unmade. Could elective reason wish for the reconstruction? And yet it is quite certain that the best of us is in the state of survival. We live in what we have done—in the idea, which seems to me the parent fountain of life, as opposed to that of perishable blood. I see all around me how much idea governs, and therein see the Creator; that other life to which we are drawn, not conscious as our sensations demand, but possibly cognizant, as the brain may now sometimes, when the blood is not too forcibly pressing on it, dimly apprehend.

Finally, in a letter of 1901 he warns against the common misconceptions of our fellow creatures:

We have to know that we know ourselves. . . . In truth so well do we know ourselves that there is a general resolve to know someone else instead. We set up an ideal of the cherished object; we try our friends and the world by the standards we have raised within, supported by pride, obscured by the passions. But if we determine to know ourselves, we see that it has been open to us all along, that in fact we did but would not know, from having such an adoration of the ideal creature erected and painted by us. It follows that, having come to this knowledge, we have the greater charity with our fellows—especially with the poor fellow exposed to our inspection.

Armed with these observations we may proceed to a closer look at Meredith's novels. But he reminds us: "I do not make a plot. If my characters as I have them at heart before I begin on them, were boxed into a plot they would soon lose the lines of their features" (*Letters of George Meredith*). Perhaps it is fair to give a last word to E. M. Forster, not a great Meredith admirer.

A Meredith plot resembles a series of kiosks most artfully placed among wooded slopes, which his people reach by their own impetus, and from which they emerge with altered aspect. Incident springs out of character, and, having occurred it alters that character. (*Aspects of the Novel*)

————

The Ordeal of Richard Feverel (1859) was Meredith's first important novel, and there have been critics who have maintained it to be his finest. Certainly it contains some of his finest prose. I vividly recall now, at age eighteen, that I was dazzled by the lyrical descriptions of the sylvan romance by the stream between the handsome young baronet's son, Richard, and the lovely farmer's niece, Lucy. And I remember as well my sympathy with the violent character of the rebellious but confused and misled hero, an idealist shorn of ideals. But the novel has fared less well with time. For its principal purpose is to disclose the madness and folly of an educational scheme whose madness and folly are patently clear to the reader from the first chapter.

Sir Austin Feverel, wealthy baronet and squire of a vast acreage, lord of an obsequious household of poor relatives and old retainers, is willfully determined to raise his only son and heir, Richard, to be a perfect gentleman, in the highest sense of that word, the cynosure of all eyes, free of the least tint of sin, who will be matched with the perfect wife—to be selected, of course, by his guardian parent. Fortunately for the project, there is no mother to interfere—Lady Feverel has fled with a poet lover. The boy will be sent to no contaminating school, nor subjected to any contaminating company. He will be educated entirely by carefully chosen tutors, and his roamings restricted to the plentiful family estates and the immediate neighborhood. Of course, Richard grows up with the high temper and lofty pride of a finely bred hound who has been taught obedience to and love for only one master; the rest of the world bows and scrapes.

Unaware of his own frustrations, he is profoundly shaken by the explosion of the first eruption of his senses: when he haps upon the beautiful Lucy by the stream. Violently in love, he thrusts aside the paternal objections, escapes to London, and marries the girl. But as he is completely dependent financially on his father, whom, despite that father's opposition, he still loves, he is obliged to negotiate with him, and his timid little wife, anxious to reconcile with her powerful father-in-law, insists that they live temporarily apart until Sir Austin shall be placated.

Richard, giving in to her plea, finds himself alone in London, and, being unschooled in the resistance of temptation, soon finds himself in the clutches of a designing demimondaine. When he learns, however, of the attempted seduction of his wife in his absence by a dissolute peer, he fights a duel with him and is gravely wounded. Recovering, he is too ashamed of himself to return to his bride, but hearing that she has given birth to a son, he rushes to her side, only to have her die of a brain fever brought on by her anxiety over him.

So Richard is punished in the end for the folly of his father's crazy educational plan. What have we to learn from such a parable? At least, anyway, we have been entertained throughout with wit and vivid characterizations.

The eponymous hero of *Evan Harrington* (1861) is an appropriate one for a Victorian novel: he is handsome, stalwart, brave, good-natured, with a charming manner and a good sense of humor, at home with the high and the humble; but he is also the son of a tailor. This fact is very important; indeed, it is what the whole book is about. His recently deceased father, Melchisedec, has been not only a tailor, but a magnificent one as well, a hearty sportsman with the air of a marquis, for which he was sometimes taken, a tradesman who actually hobnobbed with nobility, a legend in his home town of Lymport (Portsmouth). But his three daughters, however adoring, were deeply mortified to be the offspring of a (detested word!) "snip." One is married to a marine officer who won't allow her to mention her parents; another, to a kindly brewer who has been emotionally bludgeoned by the second daughter into ignoring them, and the third to a Portuguese count, Saldar, who has never even been informed of their existence. The manipulations of the three, particularly the countess, to keep the world in ignorance of their affiliation with the paternal shop in Lymport form the central theme of the novel.

Of course, in an era of far fewer avenues of communication than our own, such a concealment was more feasible, but even so the reader cannot quite believe that the daughters could be even so mildly successful in obliterating the social stain of tailordom as they are shown to be. Their pretensions are too gross. Such a turn of events, however, is always allowable in comedy, in which unlikelihood is almost a requirement, but here the trouble is that the comic sometimes jars with Meredith's serious purpose of exposing the sordid aspect of snobbery. Snobbery is by no means always funny, and I recall Oscar Wilde's trenchant observation in *A Woman of No Importance:* "To be in society is simply a bore; to be out of it is simply a tragedy." Meredith's novel, however, is always sharply alive and amusing, even if the constantly struck note of the aristocracy's contempt for trade becomes monotonous.

Evan, the hero, is not ashamed of his father's trade, but he has spent much time is Lisbon in the delightful company of his charming sister, the countess, and has no wish to expose her to the world she is trying to dupe. Besides, he has fallen in love with an English girl of high birth, Rose Jocelyn, who professes a great scorn of tradesmen, and he sees no point in creating hurdles in his path to her heart. But when he joins his bereaved mother, a splendid and rigid old woman who despises her daughters' false shame of their father, and learns that the only practical way of paying the paternal debts is to take over and run the family shop, he sturdily agrees to do so, even at the cost of abandoning a preferred diplomatic career.

The rest of the typically complex Meredith plot involves the difficulties of Evan's courtship of the aristocratic Rose, in which he is both aided and hampered by the adroit but overreaching maneuvers of his supposed ally, the countess. He is too honest and independent totally to hide his trade from the sneering young males of the Jocelyn house party, but he is also too enamored to risk damning himself in the eyes of his beloved by blurting out the whole truth to the prejudiced Rose. And in the end he comes near to ruining himself in everybody's eyes by taking the wrong position in one of those moral dilemmas that seem to give Meredith so much more trouble than they do his readers.

This is what happens. His sister the countess, in an effort to discredit a stubbornly retentive beau of Rose and remove him from her brother's matrimonial path, forges a letter in the beau's handwriting, warning the maniacally jealous and absent husband of the philandering of his wife, a guest of the Jocelyns, which brings about a savage encounter. The letter is shown; the beau is disgraced. But Evan, finding that his sister is the culprit, demands that she exonerate the beau, and when she refuses, showing herself in her true colors, he takes the blame for the letter on himself.

I believe that Meredith thought this the act of a true gentleman. But could it truly be the duty of such to ruin his own reputation and scotch all hope of future happiness, not to mention causing the misery of the girl who is at last fully in love with him and ready to forget the tailoring, to cover for a sister so vile? I think not.

But of course all is made clear in the end; boy gets girl, and Evan, happily united to Rose and her fortune, can give up tailoring and adopt a diplomatic career which will surely take him to the top of the social ladder that seemed unscalable to a "snip."

Returning to the question of Meredith's seeming contradiction between the revelations of this novel and his own personal reticence on the subject of his background, I suggest that he may have been not so much ashamed of the tailors in his family tree as disinclined to be identified with them. His nature was a romantic one; he was a poet, a friend of Swinburne and Rossetti; he loved the trappings of an old and established society of birth and wealth, however liberal his political views. What had such things to do with the busy shop of a snip where bellies and buttocks were measured with tape? He may not have scorned the family trade; he simply turned away from it. He had always essentially educated and developed himself without family aid, except from his mother's small fortune which did not come from tailoring. What did he owe to the paternal past?

Rhoda Fleming (1865) is the sad but powerfully related tale of the seduction of Dahlia Fleming, a farmer's daughter, by Edward Blancome, the son of the local squire, and the hunting down of the seducer by Robert Armstrong, the violent but stouthearted lover of the victim's sister, Rhoda. Dahlia Fleming does not elicit much sympathy for her mishap from the reader; she has agreed to become the kept mistress of Blancome under a promise of marriage which she is too well educated not to have seen as insincere. But Armstrong, a sturdy ex-alcoholic (subject to an occasional relapse) who works on her father's farm and silently but faithfully adores her sister Rhoda, is a highly sympathetic character who bluntly and relentlessly overcomes every obstacle flung in his way by the villain, including a treacherous night assault which almost kills him. I cannot fathom why the Victorian critic William Watson should have written of him: "A more thoroughly uncompanionable and unimaginative young man the writer does not remember to have met, even in real life." Perhaps Armstrong was too crude for nineteenth-century delicacy.

At any rate, the stricken Dahlia is brought home, repentant, and Armstrong at last wins his Rhoda. But there are none of Meredith's curious moral twists at the end. A rustic wretch has been purchased to give Dahlia the wedded status required by the country neighbors, and she is about to wed this horror when the villain Edward turns up, inexplicably (Meredith never satisfies us about this), having had a change of heart and offers to marry the woman he has so cruelly wronged. And Rhoda opposes him! She takes a high moral stand against any compromise with her sister's seducer, even though he is rich, able, and repentant, and Dahlia still loves him! So Dahlia, breaking under her sister's righteous preaching, marries the sorry clot of a bought spouse, who promptly after the ceremony turns nasty. The miserable bride, turning now on Rhoda, reviles her in a tensely dramatic scene. But the damage is done. Rhoda realizes her mistake and in her sorrow is rewarded with the hand and love of the faithful Armstrong. But did Meredith ever realize he had turned his heroine into a monster? I doubt it.

The novel, like all of Meredith's, has a host of minor characters, some of whom are depicted with the vivid realism that always goes—a bit oddly at times—hand-in-hand with Meredith's powerfully evocative descriptions of nature, so that the characters seem to be seen like brightly colored insects against a glorious foliage. Sometimes, however, Meredith falls into the trap that Dickens set for his contemporaries by delineating a minor character with a single characteristic and showing that trait over and over. This tendency has the danger of becoming wearisome in all writers but Dickens, and even at times, be it whispered, with him. Anthony Hackbut, the old bachelor uncle of Dahlia and Rhoda, is a sorry example of this kind of portrayal. His job is to transport bullion through the streets of London from or to his bank employer; obviously he has to be a thoroughly trusted porter. His whole life is premised on his sense of the importance of his function, which is never absent from his mind or his lips. But he ends up a thief, although he believes that his crime is for a good cause. And he is a bore.

––––––––

The remarkable thing about the remarkable novel *Beauchamp's Career* (1875) is that one's sympathy for its attractive but blundering hero never wavers throughout its many, perhaps a few too many, pages. Nevil Beauchamp starts out with every trump in the hand he has been dealt. He is gloriously handsome, a Crimean War hero, with a generous heart and a stout ambition to alleviate, where he can, the misery of the human condition, and he is the beloved nephew and presumed heir of a crusty and rich aristocratic bachelor uncle, the Honorable Everard Romfrey. Yet everything goes wrong for him, sometimes by bad luck, but more often through his own stubborn and at times quixotic adherence to a private and rigid moral code.

He falls in love with a beautiful French girl of noble birth, Renée, who has been pledged by her father to an elderly marquis, and loses her. This is bad luck. Years later, when she flees from her husband to London, he is on the verge of running off to Italy with her, but her husband's successful recapture of her prevents the escape. This is good luck. He then becomes the devoted and uncritical disciple of an old republican radical, who, however sincerely passionate over the plight of the masses, is a ranting bore, thus alienating his uncle and most of his friends, to no effective purpose. When his violent uncle takes it upon himself almost to thrash the life out of the poor old radical, Doctor Schrapnel, Beauchamp devotes the major efforts of his lifetime to the task of inducing his uncle to apologize. This is folly, for what possible good does it do for anyone, including Schrapnel? But we love Beauchamp for it. Then he courts a beautiful heiress, with whom he is in love and whose fortune he now desperately needs for his political future, but he manages with exaggerated honesty to convince her that he will make a hopeless husband, and she leaves him for a steadier man.

In the end Beauchamp at last extracts an apology from his uncle, but only by arousing the latter's pity because of a grave illness through which he is devotedly nursed by Schrapnel's loving niece, whom he afterwards lovelessly, but gratefully, marries. Finally he is drowned rescuing a little boy from the sea. This is certainly bad luck. At the close of the novel the two enemies, Doctor Schrapnel and Beauchamp's uncle, gaze upon the abashed little creature whose life their disciple and nephew has saved.

This is what we have in exchange for Beauchamp.

It was not uttered but it was visible in the blank stare at one another of the two men who loved Beauchamp, after they had examined the insignificant bit of mudbank life remaining in this world in the place of him.

There are those who have seen snobbishness in these last lines. I do not so read them. I see them more in the light of the ending of *Tess of the d'Urbervilles* by Meredith's friend Hardy: "The president of the immortals had finished his sport with Tess." Obviously, Meredith was offering no clue as to why the boy was spared and Beauchamp lost. He was only concerned with showing a man who could be as fine as he was futile. Beauchamp has accomplished little enough in his life, but he has left a glow. We must content ourselves with this. Who knows what that insignificant bit of mudbank, life, may not accomplish?

Opinion for and against the novel may be summarized in the following quotations. The first is from Arthur Symons's review of *Beauchamp's Career.*

Nevil Beauchamp, whose career, political and domestic, the story treats of, is one of the most admirably drawn of Mr. Meredith's heroes, and I think intrinsically the noblest in nature of them all. His strange, attractive character with its fiery sincerity, its dashing and determined impulsiveness, its tenacity of will and temerity of purpose, is represented with spirit, but always sympathetic impartiality. The story of his career is saddening, in the contrast of so splendid a nature, and so small an appreciable result; such gifts for happiness, and so troubled a life, so tragic a death.

The second is from the American critic W. C. Brownell.

Even when such favorites of his [Meredith's] own as Nevil Beauchamp are concerned, he is almost timorous lest your tenderness should be unintelligent. This is carried so far that one rarely cares much what becomes of these personages. You know in advance that they will never be the sport of any spontaneity. Their fate is sealed. They are the slaves of their creator's will, counters in his game. And this is why, in playing it, though he constantly challenges our admiration, he does not hold our interest. The air of free agency that he throws around them does not deceive us. We don't at all know what is to befall them, how they are going to act, but we have an ever-present sense that they are going to act, but we have an ever-present sense that he does, and this sense is only sharpened by the knowledge, born of experience in reading his books, that he is going to make them surprise us. (J. A. Hammenter, *George Meredith, His Life and Art in Anecdote and Criticism*)

The Adventures of Harry Richmond (1871) seems to me to have the faults of *Beauchamp's Career* without its virtues. Yet it was the first really popular book that Meredith published. Such popularity seems unaccountable today. It is the rambling picaresque tale of Richmond Roy and his son, the former a man who ridiculously claims to be the legitimate, as opposed to the bastard, son of a royal British duke and an actress, and who spends a futile lifetime and the money of everyone he can fleece in a vain effort to establish what he shrilly calls his rights. He has once won the love of the daughter of a fabulously wealthy English squire and driven her with his vagaries to a premature and lunatic death, he lays claim to his son Harry, who has been raised by the devoted old maternal grandfather who intends to make him his heir. Roy's legal claim is good, and Harry is taken off to his father's London home.

In the first chapters a rather rollicking pace is maintained as we follow Harry's boyhood, schooling and early loves, sometimes with Roy and sometimes with the squire, until, travelling in Europe in search of his mysteriously absent father, Harry meets and falls in love with Ottilia, daughter of the reigning prince of a minor German state. And here the story lags atrociously.

As the critic George Parsons Lathrop put it in his *George Meredith:*

> The story breaks down utterly in the middle. Continual hammering on one
> line of effect dulls the edge. The length of the narrative, too, the multitude
> of persons introduced, and their all but endless involvements tax the atten-
> tion beyond endurance. Yet the unabated energy with which old Roy,
> gradually developing into insanity in his schemes for recognition by the
> royal family, is kept before us, stimulates even a tired brain; and Harry's slow
> evolution from blind love and worship of his father to a perception of his
> real worthless, erratic and scoundrelly character shoots through the whole
> an intensely vivid and pathetic ray of light.

Where the book differs so peculiarly from *Beauchamp's Career* is that Harry
shows himself a gullible ass from start to finish, yet ends up being rewarded
with the hand and immense fortune of the lovely and loving cousin whom
he has long scorned and whom his exasperated grandfather has at last substi-
tuted for him in his will. Unlike Beauchamp he gets everything he has willfully repudiated.

It should have been evident to Harry from the first day when he had to
spring his father from debtors' jail that his parent was unreliable and untrust-
worthy. And after that he has numerous opportunities to see just how vile
Roy can be. But even after this becomes clear to him, his loyalty is unshaken,
and he does not hesitate to alienate his loving grandfather, pour his last cent
into the paternal grasp, and abandon all idea of a serious career to stay near
Roy, except when he enters parliament through a rotten borough. Even his
supposed love for the princess Ottilia (he ultimately makes an easy recovery)
is a sequel to his father's ambition for him, and for a long time he tolerates
Roy's unscrupulous cultivation of Ottilia's father. And yet there is nothing
wrong with Harry's mind. The novel is shaped in the form of a memoir in
which he is the "I," and we are treated to the subtlety and wit of his cogita-
tions. His continued servitude to a scoundrel is ultimately disgusting.

Of course, the father has charm; that is necessary to sustain the novel and
any of a reader's credibility in Harry. And he loves his son in his own way—
largely as an extension of himself and his own self-created legend. He hopes
that Harry, wed to a princess and heir to a fortune, will be a very great man.
This to Roy justifies any ruse, any deception. One ultimately tires of his mere
shoddiness. And the princess, unlike almost any other heroine of Meredith,
is a cold statue of a woman, utterly unreal, fit only to be drawn by the deft
pencil of George du Maurier who illustrated the first edition.

Nonetheless, the English public bought the novel in quantities. And Edith Wharton wrote in her memoirs that she treasured it.

———

Sandra Belloni (1864), first published as *Emilia in England,* and its sequel, *Vittoria,* deal essentially with the Italian Risorgimento and fall into their own category in Meredith's fiction. In 1865 he had been sent to the Italian front as a war reporter of the conflict with Austria, and he had observed the fighting and the devastation and had made particular note of the bitter rivalries and jealousies between the loosely united Italian principalities, which were not to bury their differences until the ultimate victory of 1870. But he chose for his two Italian novels the earlier era of 1848–1849 when Lombardy and Venice, once part of the Italian Republic created by Napoleon but ceded to Austria by the Treaty of Vienna, had rebelled unsuccessfully against the Hapsburg emperor in uneasy alliance with Charles Albert, the king of Sardinia, who was widely distrusted. Milan provides the center of action for both novels; it seethes with radicals who resent the House of Savoy, with royalists who support it, with street crowds who bait and defy the Austrian soldiers, and with wealthy collaborationists who take their orders from Vienna.

The more sympathetic characters are the Italian patriots who are passionately opposed to the Austrian rule and willing, even eager, to die in pursuit of national liberty. And Meredith is clearly on their side. Yet he is always fair in delineating the Austrian occupiers and even the less patriotic Italians who more or less clandestinely support them. Indeed, some of his most vivid characterizations are found among the latter. Captain Weisspreiss of the Austrian army, the expert swordsman who slaughters in duels all the Lombardian officers who dare to challenge him—for even in wartime private duels between enemy officers are sanctioned—is something of a brute who is determined to marry a fortune, but he is also a gentleman good to his word and strictly honorable according to his military code. Count Serabiglione is Meredith's brilliant sketch of a rich collaborationist who successfully seeks the solid comforts of two mutually hostile worlds, and the Countess Violetta is an alluring and splendidly evil spy. Meredith paints a lurid but convincing picture of a beautiful and ancient city riddled with hate and suspicion but occasionally radiating with the glow of self-sacrifice.

And to top all this he has created the character of Sandra Belloni, later called Vittoria Campa, the great diva whose heart is given to the cause of Italian freedom and unification. Some critics have claimed that Meredith has given us in her the classic portrait of a great and dedicated artist. I doubt this. He offers us no real study of the long and arduous training of a great voice as does Willa Cather in *The Song of the Lark* or even Marcia Davenport in *Of Lena Geyer.* All we learn is that Vittoria is a richly vibrant contralto and that she deeply treasures her gift from the gods. But she doesn't treat it as do other divas, notorious for their driving ambition and their ego. She is easily diverted from her operatic career by her passion for the handsome, courageous, but morally loose Pierson, and the only person who keeps her nose to the grindstone, so to speak, is the Greek millionaire opera buff, Mr. Pericles, who is willing to kidnap her to guard her from the distractions of love and war. And in the end, as the exalted widow of the slain hero Carlo Ammiani, she gives up singing altogether to rear their little son, except for the single occasion when she joins in the triumphant Te Deum that celebrates the victory in 1870. Is that like any diva one has heard of?

Yet as a character she fascinates, enough so to hold the reader's attention through two novels, although the pace of the story doesn't really pick up until the scene is shifted from London to Milan. Sandra may end up a countess, married into an ancient Milanese family, but she starts her career in a London slum, the only child of an impoverished and exiled Italian musician and his simple and subservient wife, and her talent is discovered only by chance when she is heard singing at night on a farm where she has been sent to work in the neighborhood of the Poles, a rich bourgeois family with a big suburban villa. The three Pole sisters semi-adopt her, thinking she will be an asset in their social climbing, and she attracts the impassioned attentions of the Greek opera buff who determines to launch her on her career. Pure, simple, noble-natured, taking the world at face value, and cultivating her gift of song, Sandra is sublimely unconscious of the smallness and snobbishness of the Pole sisters and is quite happy until she falls in love with their brother, Wilfred Pole, later to take the name of an uncle, Pierson.

Pierson returns her love passionately but he knows he cannot afford to marry her—his father's financial state is precarious, and besides, he is engaged to an older lady of noble birth. Sandra continues to believe in her lover even after his duplicity has been revealed to her, and wanders about the streets of London, at night and alone, perilously close to suicide. She is rescued, however—almost every man in the book who meets her falls in love with her—and is sent off to Milan by the rich Mr. Pericles to study voice. But once again she is distracted from her true career by her immediate and rhapsodic adoption of the cause of Italian freedom and agrees, in her first operatic role, to sing the patriotic aria that will trigger a planned revolt.

From this point on the action of the novel becomes swift and gripping; one can see why *Vittoria* was the precursor of such romantic tales as H. Rider Haggard's *King Solomon's Mines* and Anthony Hope's *The Prisoner of Zenda*. The are duels, chases, and hairbreadth escapes, assassinations and battle scenes. And through it all Vittoria remains cool, serene, uncompromising in what she deems her line of duty. She is also a bit of a goose; Meredith is uncompromising in his determination to delineate all sides of a character. She allows her impulse to warn visiting English friends of possible danger, even at the risk of exposing the revolt, and she insists on sounding her signal for the public uprising even after she has been told the coup has been postponed. She also disobeys the command of her beloved, the rebel hero Count Carlo Ammiani, to come to his side on the excuse that she must tend a wounded friend. But Meredith manages to endow her with a fineness of spirit and a charm that ultimately subdues criticism.

It is surely a fault in the structure of the novel that he draws the curtain over Ammiani's preliminary courtship of Vittoria. We must simply accept the fact that the two have fallen deeply in love. The count is shown as heroic and handsome, totally dedicated to his betrothed and his cause, but we never see him in the earlier stages of love-making, and Vittoria's idolization of his memory after his death—which is really a kind of stylish suicide—is sentimental and even mawkish. There is little in the book to indicate that the failed revolt of 1848, which caused so much slaughter, contributed much to the ultimate defeat of Austria.

It is curious that the English characters in the novel are so much flatter than the Italians or Austrians. Methyr Powys, who without adequate explanation volunteers to fight with the Milanese, and his almost maniacally devoted sister, are hollow beings; the Pole sisters, like some Dickens people, consist entirely of one quality, their snobbishness; their father is simply a fool, and his lady friend, the vulgar Irish widow Chump, a creature of farce. Captain Gambier is too vaguely drawn to be understood; only Wilfred Pole, renamed Pierson, is interesting.

Like many principal Meredith characters he is endowed with contradictions, seemingly relegating him more to life than to fiction. Indeed a reader's recognition of this is one of the needed keys to appreciating Meredith. Pierson is the Pole brother who deserts the young Sandra Belloni, but her unsought revenge is terrible: he never recovers from the emotion she has aroused in him. It destroys two of his ambitious engagements: first his betrothal to the daughter of an English peer and, second, to an Austrian heiress. To nurse his unavailing love for Vittoria, or simply to live near her, becomes his main occupation in life, effectively cutting his military and social careers into ribbons. Although he has joined the army of Austria, where an uncle of his from whom he expects favors is a general, he doesn't hesitate to betray his adopted flag by favoring the escape of an enemy prisoner befriended by his beloved. Reduced in rank to a private soldier, he yet fights so bravely and recklessly that he recovers his lieutenancy. At all points in his story his courage and skill with arms is contrasted with his weakness of character, and his essential egotism with his sense of pity even for the women he wrongs. He is small-minded, sometimes mean, curiously honest with himself, almost sympathetic. Where would you meet him except in Meredith? Or in life.

———

The Egoist (1879) has all the tightness of plot and concentration in time and action of a tragedy by Racine. The scene is limited to Sir Willoughby Patterne's baronial manor and estate, where all the characters are either resident or visiting, or to which they are near neighbors, and the beautiful surrounding countryside of Sir Willoughby's extended acres gives Meredith the occasion for some of his finest rural descriptions. And the time of the action is limited to a couple of weeks, from the arrival of Clara Middleton and her clerical father for a prenuptial visit to her baronet fiancé, to the ultimate breaking of her engagement, the story of which is the whole and adequate plot of the novel.

We meet Clara at her first and fatal moment of doubt as to the wisdom of her plighted troth. Sir Willoughby at first has struck her as everything a young woman could desire, even such a surpassingly lovely young woman as we at once see her to be. He is handsome, elegant, athletic, intelligent, of gracious manners, large fortune, and ancient ancestry, in short, the idol of the county. He is also very much in love with her. His mother, his aunts, the whole neighborhood applaud the match; all arms are stretched out to greet Clara. Her father approves; her large dowry is settled and her bridesmaids chosen; the air rings with welcome.

But it has begun to dawn horridly upon her that she has pledged herself to an egoist whose sole inner concern is the worship of himself and that she has been chosen to be the leader of the choir whose essential function will be to sing anthems in his praise throughout eternity. Willoughby has even gone so far as to ask her to vow that, if widowed, she will never stain his posthumous glory by taking a second mate.

The modern reader must accept the fact that in 1879 the more conservative elements of English society considered an engagement almost as binding as marriage itself and that it could be properly broken only by mutual consent. The problem treated in *The Egoist* is that Willoughby refuses to release his betrothed even after she has told him flatly that her love for him is dead. He still wants her as a trophy, and the unfortunate girl believes that she is bound, unless she can somehow induce him to free her. Her frantic search for a way is the theme of the novel.

What is most poignant and sobering in the story is that Clara is at all times surrounded by people who either love her or are dazzled by her. Her widower father beams on his only child, at least so long as she doesn't upset him; Vernon Whitfield, Sir Willoughby's poor relation and secretary, is moodily in love with her; Laetitia Dale, the lovelorn and impoverished spinster, is critical but basically sympathetic to her; Mrs. Mountstuart Jenkinson, the local grande dame, greatly admires her; Hector de Craye, Willoughby's Irish best man, like Vernon, is smitten by her; the baronet's maiden aunts solemnly adore her. And Willoughby himself, however vindictive he becomes at her falling off, craves her even as a reluctant bride. But they all respect the binding force of her given word. They may think Willoughby *should* release her, but if he won't, well . . . Hector de Craye is the only one who thinks she should break away, willy-nilly, but he doesn't care about the rights and wrongs of the matter; he wants her for himself. He doesn't know, of course, that she is beginning to fall in love with Vernon.

Clara has only one weapon to use in her struggle for liberty, but it is a formidable one: her radiating charm. She is the loveliest of Meredith's heroines. She is a beautiful butterfly in a gilded cage, and the desperate beating of her wings against the walls of her prison of kindness lends a kind of grimness to the ineffective will that she so successfully and futilely evokes.

But as fate seems to be closing in on the poor girl we begin to see the other characters in a darker light. Are they really willing to consign Clara to a wretched life for the sake of a convention in which they really cannot more than half believe?

Willoughby's self love eats up his very soul and renders him at last capable of the vilest deception. His egotism begins to betray itself in the tone of his voice and the falseness of his professed ideals; it ultimately stains his very countenance. And Vernon, though ultimately the hero and winner of Clara, is for a long time semi-paralyzed by his sense of the wrong that she has even innocently done his cousin and almost willfully exaggerates what he deems her flirting with de Craye. Dr. Middleton shows himself a pompous pedant willing to sacrifice his daughter for the sake of his future son-in-law's incomparable wine cellar. Mrs. Mountstuart Jenkinson cannot understand how any young woman would allow any obstacle to prevent her becoming mistress of Patterne Hall; the Patterne aunts cannot believe that anyone could fall out of love with their nephew; even Laetitia Dale shudders at the idea of love withdrawn, and, as for de Craye, he is only for stealing the bride for himself. There is even a sense that the author, for all his admiration of his enchanting puppet, knits his brow a bit at Clara's folly in engaging herself to a man she knew so little.

In the end it is only through a bit of luck that Clara is released from her vow. A deus ex machina intervenes when Willoughby, fearing that Clara may escape him after all, tries to cover the shame of a jilting by claiming that he is the jilter, and proposes to Laetitia Dale, his old flame, only be turned down! But he is overheard by his poor relative, the boy Crossjay Patterne, concealed under the cushions of a divan, who is devoted to Clara and spreads the news, so that when Willoughby, unsuccessful in his search for an alternative mate, returns to the his remorseless pursuit of Clara, she is able to confront him with his apostasy and gain her freedom.

And supposing this had not happened? Meredith towards the end shows Clara as almost broken in spirit. Would she have been dragged to the altar? One can imagine her fleeing back down the aisle, just before the final uniting words are spoken, her wedding veil streaming behind her. The boy Crossjay, the god from the machine, provides a better ending.

It is a great novel. Meredith was never more successful in activating what he calls the imps of comedy waiting to pounce on mortals who deceive themselves. But under the beauty of Patterne Hall and the rural countryside, under all the wit and good manners of the clever and genteel persons who foregather in the halls and on the lawns, lies the immediate possibility of a life lost for a violation of a simple form.

Meredith made important use of two episodes in the life of the famous Caroline Norton, granddaughter of the playwright Richard Brinsley Sheridan, in constructing his plot for *Diana of the Crossways*. When Mrs. Norton was twenty-eight in 1836, her husband, the Honorable George, brought a suit against the prime minister, Lord Melbourne, for seduction of his wife. The jury exonerated the distinguished defendant without leaving the box; the baseless and vindictive suit was generally believed to have been politically motivated. Later, in 1846, a rumor, apparently false, was widely circulated that Mrs. Norton had sold to the *London Times* a political secret confided to her by a friend, namely that Sir Robert Peel had decided to reverse his support of the Corn Laws, which prohibited the export or import of grain.

In the novel the heroine Diana Merion Warwick faces a similar law suit over her friendship with Lord Dannisburgh, and her husband is similarly non-suited. It is made clear to the reader that her relationship with the elderly peer has been an innocent one. But unlike Mrs. Norton, Diana *is* guilty of selling a political secret to a London newspaper. Mrs. Norton had died eight years before the publication of *Diana of the Crossways* in 1885, but her surviving sister, Lady Dufferin, was incensed that so low an act should have been even by implication attributed to her sibling, and Meredith had to insert a note in all subsequent editions of the book stating that the work was purely fictional and no libel intended.

Mrs. Norton's story was a dramatic one, and it provided fine fodder for Meredith's genius, but the episode of the sale to the newspaper has given many readers considerable trouble. Would the woman he created really have been capable of selling an important secret confided to her by the man she loved? I think not.

We meet Diana Merion, a radiantly beautiful orphan of nineteen, half Irish, half English, with a mind and wit sharp to the point of brilliance, fresh, idealistic, hopeful of great things in the future, at a ball in Dublin. She has little wealth, but her father was a soldier and a hero, and she should be able to choose a husband from among the best in the British Isles. The world seems to be at her feet, but her head is not turned. A persistent realist, despite all her fantasies, she is poignantly aware of the economic plight of Ireland and of its servitude to an unsympathetic parliament in London, and she is already fully conscious that her high ambitions as a woman may well be blocked by the arrogance and possessiveness of the Victorian male. Diana may be a shining light, but she sees very clearly the darker objects that she illuminates. And she knows that her kind of vision is resented by those it exposes. There are plenty of men—and of women, too—who are eager to stamp out the light in which they are viewed only too well.

Nowhere else in Meredith's fiction is a principal character more success-fully identified with Nature, whose beauty over the downs of the south coast of England echoes and intensifies the beauty of Diana in body and soul. We are constantly being raised up over the jealousies and bickerings of a mali-ciously gossiping London society by Meredith's invocation of the winds, the rains, the clouds and all of the magnificent vegetation of the rural country-side. Diana's share of the glory of the seasons enhances her intrinsic dignity. Any number of instances of Meredith's success with scenic description could be given; one may suffice.

> They drove out immediately after breakfast, on one of those high morn-ings of the bared bosom of June, and a soft air fondles leaf and grassblade, and beauty and peace are overheard, reflected, if we will. Rain had fallen in the night. Here and there hung a milk white cloud with folded sail. The Southwest left it in its bay of blue, and breathed below. At moments the fresh scent of herb and mould swung richly in warmth. The young beech trees glittered, pools of rainwater made the roadways laugh, the grass banks under hedges rolled their interwoven weeds in cascades of many shaded green to the right and left of the pair of dappled ponies, and a squirrel crossed ahead, a lark went up a little way to ease its heart, closing his wings when the burst was over.

Diana is an independent soul, without parent or sibling, and she spends long visits with her dearest friend and soul mate, Emma Dunstane, the slightly older rich wife of a baronet ex-soldier. The friendship, movingly de-scribed, is the one anchor in the younger woman's restless life, and when she is subjected to a clumsy pass by Emma's essentially well meaning but sadly lecherous husband, she flees the house in horror. Indeed, so great is her disillusionment with men, that she violently overreacts and seeks the seeming safety of a sudden marriage to Mr. Warwick, a stiff but apparently proper gentleman of leisure, many years her senior, who offers what she takes to be a secure and dignified life of comparative tranquility. But she soon finds that she has chained herself to a cold and vindictive egoist who can-not even share her love of art and letters. And so she makes the first of many almost fatal mistakes, attributable to her nervous compulsion immediately to rectify one mistake with another. She falls in love with a brilliant young nobleman, Percy Dacier, a rising politician, with whom, of course, she can-not wed.

Diana was one of Meredith's favorite heroines, and none, even the enchanting Clara Middleton of *The Egoist* is more attractive; certainly none is wittier. Indeed, one can well understand why her rapier sharpness makes her enemies among the less enlightened. She was "one of the women dear to me," Meredith wrote; she even "sat beside him" at the burial service of one of his dearest friends, "and he gave her to me" (*Letters of George Meredith*).

Perhaps that is why he becomes as her creator almost too fiercely her advocate. He seems to find Percy Dacier cold and unfeeling in refusing to forgive Diana, his beloved, whom he plans to marry after the death of her ailing and separated husband, for selling to the press a vital cabinet secret that he has confided to her in a passionate love scene. Indeed, she has gone, so to speak, straight from his arms to the newspaper office at midnight! It is a blind spot in Meredith not to see that this might well be enough to alienate the most ardent lover.

————

One of Our Conquerors (1891)—the title referring ironically to financial magnates as Britain's new ruling class—was published after Meredith had achieved a wide circulation as well as critical acclaim, and it marked a change in his style with a denser weaving of author comment into the delineation of characters and a more complicated and occasionally obscure phraseology. Henry James complained to Edith Wharton that, when he read the Meredith of this period, "He was at a loss to know where he was, or what causes led to which events, or even by what form of conveyance the elusive characters he was struggling to identify moved from one point of the globe to another" (*A Backward Glance*). The novel has proved something of a stumbling block to would-be admirers of Meredith, despite the claims of his more devoted fans that it is one of his finest.

I am afraid that I could not recommend it to any reader today. It is not that the cause of the "fallen" woman, victimized by a society adopting the double standard, has ceased to be a moral issue. We readily enough adapt ourselves to a long bygone reverence for the binding force of a betrothal in *The Egoist*. It is more that Meredith, for all his trumpeting about the cruel discrimination against an unfortunate woman, cannot engender much sympathy for Victor Radnor and his lover, Nataly, who are unable to legalize their two decades of "living in sin" because of the adamant refusal of Victor's wife to divorce him. Victor as a young and penniless man has married an elderly widow for her money and eloped with Nataly, her beautiful paid companion.

He has subsequently made a huge fortune, sired a lovely daughter, Nesta, and now yearns to enter a society that will not tolerate such a liaison as his. So he lies about it, builds a palace, and tries to lure fashionable London into it. As one contemporary critic said of the novel, it is like trying to make a hero out of a man who cheated at cards.

It has been argued that the complex details with which the principal characters are studied are necessary to understand their sometimes seemingly illogical acts: that Meredith is creating real as opposed to fictional people who are, of course, much less simple and direct. Victor and Nataly are seen a hundred times over in their dialogue, their actions, and their innermost thoughts (an early use of the stream of consciousness). But they still emerge as the simple souls we would have comprehended in a small fraction of the words their creator expends on them.

Victor is a complacent, self-satisfied, and rather vulgarly extravagant millionaire, with a parcel of decent qualities. He is generous and kindly to the little court that his wealth attracts; he is a charitable and patriotic citizen: he adores his daughter and her mother, although he is given to flirting and hand-holding with a titled lady. But his life is one long lie, and he prays for the early demise of his stubborn and sickly old wife. And for all his idolization of his daughter Nesta, he conceals the fact that the man she loves has become available as a widower, which might impede her accepting the expected proposal of an earl's heir. Nataly herself has neither the need nor the desire for social recognition, but her love for him is paralyzing, and she limits herself to inward moaning rather than heartening her lover to accept their situation and brave the world. He is a fool, and she a coward. She dies in the end, and he goes mad and also dies, but to crown his ineptitudes, he manages to perish intestate, with the result that Nesta cannot, as a bastard, inherit his fortune. Happily however, she doesn't care, as she is now able to wed the man of her choice, who has adequate means. She alone is granted a happy ending.

Two-thirds of the novel is devoted to establishing the reader's understanding of the problem which Victor and Nataly face in their efforts to mislead and attract society. But the reader is perfectly aware of the problem and the unlikelihood of their success from the very beginning. Furthermore it strains his credulity that they could be even as temporarily successful as they are. At the end of the nineteenth century no man as fabulously rich as Victor could rationally hope to hoodwink a society as determined to vet the new rich—

always anyway regarded with suspicion—as the British aristocracy. And for a girl as clever and observant as Nesta to have remained so long in ignorance of her parents' non-marital situation is also unlikely.

Meredith makes much of the theme of Nature against Convention. Victor tries to persuade himself that he is fundamentally justified in favoring Nature, which has transformed his tempered inclination for a withered old mate into a passion for a fresh new one, and spurred him on to defy convention, which forbids women any sexual activity outside of marriage, but of course he hasn't defied convention at all. He has simply tried to fool it. He is in the ungracious position of wanting to have his cake and eat it too. His problem is symbolized and foretold in the first chapter when he slips while crossing London Bridge on foot and takes a tumble. He is assisted to his feet by a friendly workman who, in doing so, soils Victor's white waistcoat with his dirty hands. The ungrateful Victor remonstrates, and in the angry dispute that ensues the workman cries "None of your punctilio!" The word becomes the symbol of the futility of Victor's idle and pompous formality in talk and manner against an indignant lower class. It also demonstrates the futility of his efforts to thrust himself into a class that rejects him. His whole life is nothing but punctilio. The word occurs again and again like a Wagnerian leitmotif. It is no defense against convention. It looks itself like a papier-mâché convention.

The novel demonstrates, if further demonstration were needed, Meredith's utter inability to distinguish what is boring in his books from what is not. One of his characters insists on relating a parable entitled "The Rival Tongues," which is not only long and deadly dull, but also completely irrelevant to everything else in the book. Meredith himself was widely considered a great wit and storyteller, but I have noted that several of his friends and guests have written of their mild objection to his monopolizing the conversation with extended monologues to which his only interruption was his roars of laughter at his own jokes. You can't tell me that a man with that habit wasn't sometimes tedious. I know that many men have extolled Meredith's wit at social gatherings, but long experience with gentlemen's clubs has taught me with what patient reverence my sex will tolerate the bores that great men sometimes become.

———

Henry James, never an enthusiastic reader of Meredith's fiction, however much he admired and liked the man, was particularly hard on *Lord Ormont and His Aminta* (1894). In a letter he wrote: "I doubt if any quantity of extravagant verbiage, of airs and graces, of phrases and attitudes, of obscurities and alembications, ever stated less their subject, ever contributed less of a statement, told the reader less of what the reader needs to know." Yet however valid this might have been as a critique of the opening chapters of *One of Our Conquerors,* it is peculiarly unfair to those of *Lord Ormont and His Aminta.* Meredith seems, quite untypically, to have taken heed of the poor reception accorded to the earlier novel and to have made a conscious effort to write a more readily comprehendible book in the one that followed. And indeed Lord Ormont is a smooth, easily readable, and almost sugary romantic tale.

The plot, tightly constructed, is convincing, except for one hitch. Lord Ormont is a wealthy sexagenarian peer, a national hero, a general with a long record of brilliant military victories throughout the empire, who has lost favor with the British government by his unauthorized though successful armed crushing of an incipient Indian mutiny that the civilian administration had been attempting to quell by negotiation. Despite the overwhelming popular opinion in his favor at home and the almost inevitable ultimate restoration of his military standing, Ormont chooses to sulk like Achilles in his tent, denouncing parliament in intemperate letters to the press and spurning all efforts towards reconciliation. A lifetime bachelor, though the survivor of many tempestuous love affairs and duels, he falls in love with and weds a beautiful and noble-minded girl, several decades his junior, of small fortune and undistinguished family, and plans to lead a wandering life with her in European spas, abandoning a Britain which he feels has betrayed him. But when Aminta, at first utterly compliant to the husband whom she has long idolized as a hero, at last find the courage to suggest that they spend at least some time in England and take their part in the social life and obligations of an earl, he is irate. He will allow *her* to stay in London, yes, and support her, and even continue to love her, but he will neither acknowledge their marriage to the public nor allow her the status of a countess. That will be her punishment for not falling in with his nomadic schemes.

His true motive we do not learn until two-thirds of the tale has been told, but his cruel and arbitrary treatment of his spouse keeps our curiosity alive. The earl is splendidly drawn in all his exaggerated pride and military expertise, and in the appalling eccentricity which Victorian novelists have so often attributed to British peers. His redoubtable sister, Lady Charlotte, is more than his match in her roughness, crude honesty, and basic good sense. But what rings false in the story is Ormont's willingness to allow his wife to mingle with the tainted demimonde, which is the only society ready to receive her after he has besmirched her reputation in a cloud of doubt. It is simply inconceivable that a man of his pride and valor could have tolerated that.

Conceding this, however, on the grounds of his absolute trust of Aminta's virtue, the story hangs together. More than that, it is actually exciting. Little by little Aminta's faith in her despotic spouse is chipped away. She keeps, rather than returning, the love letters of a villainous world-be seducer; at least they offer her a glimpse of something that looks like a true affection. And gradually she allows her girlhood crush on the valiant school boy, Matthew Weyburn, who has unexpectedly reentered her life as her husband's secretary, to develop into the deep and fully returned love that was so early torn from her. Ultimately he persuades her to flee the marital yoke and live as his mistress in the school he has established in Switzerland.

Just as her love for her husband disintegrates with the new independence that his harsh conduct has engendered in her, so does Lord Ormont's love for her wax with its waning counterpart. He will acknowledge her now as his wife and seeks to cover her with the priceless family jewels, but it is too late. She has gone. And he can only survive to forgive her and offer his blessing to the adulterous pair.

Aminta and Weyburn appear to be happy running their school together; we are not told how the families of their students view the relationship between the headmaster and the fugitive countess. Meredith sometimes slips around such hurdles. Anyway, at the end we are reassured by the news that the death of the old earl has cleared the way for their legal union. The novel is a strong assertion of the basic right of an honest and honorable couple to fling off the chain of an obviously impossible and ill-considered marriage. In Meredith's long preoccupation with the struggle between Nature and Convention, Nature at last comes out on top.

Weyburn is shown as a boy totally devoted to the idolization of Lord Ormont, who is then, of course, only a distant and semilegendary figure to him, and he converts the young Aminta to his cult of the hero. Indeed her ultimate attraction to the veteran warrior may stem from her youthful attraction to his early acolyte. But there are moments in the book when the boy Weyburn seems overly obsessed with his subject, and certainly the mature Aminta is a bit of a goose to fancy herself so in love with the old soldier. And although Meredith is meticulous in revealing every flaw in the character of the surly Ormont, an underlying reverence for the British military establishment occasionally creeps out. This is also true in *Beauchamp's Career*. Meredith, for all his liberalism, for all his doubts about the justice or even the wisdom of British imperialism, had a moist eye for a man-of-war on the high seas or a fluttering Union Jack on a desert fortress. He loved a parade.

The last novel that Meredith completed, *The Amazing Marriage* (1895) repeats the theme of *Lord Ormont,* of a husband who, for no reason with which the reader can sympathize, elects to deny his thoroughly innocent and honorable lawful wife her status as such. But whereas Lord Ormont at least has the feeble excuse that Aminta has refused to fall in with his travel plans, and continues to cherish her privately, Lord Fleetwood in the later novel behaves like a brute to the lovely Carinthia simply because she has accepted a marriage proposal that he insists she should have recognized as too precipitate to be taken seriously but which he himself feels foolishly bound by. If he had simply explained this to her, she would have released him, but he has not, and she has blindly let herself believe that he was really in love with her. Throughout the story he behaves like the madman that his ultimate decision to become a monk shows him to have been, and the reader simply fails to comprehend why Meredith ever dreamed that Fleetwood's crazy meanderings would furnish material for an interesting novel. To be sure, there are splendid descriptions of Alpine scenery in the early chapters, and the character of the amusing and philosophizing Gower Woodset, reputedly based on Robert Louis Stevenson, is diverting, but these hardly make a book.

Vernon Lee, a devoted admirer of Meredith, made a desperate effort to justify this final fiction: "Here one is tempted to imagine that the seeming imperfections are only part of the excellence. Are all our aesthetics mistaken, and is it possible that the greatest written things are just those which have least literary body, which are quickest dismembered and absorbed by the reader, turned into a part of himself? . . . What we take for reality, may be in the higher walks of literature, the recognition of what our soul requires" (Sassoon, *George Meredith*).

Siegfried Sassoon, quite rightly in my opinion, would have none of this. Commenting on this passage of Vernon Lee's he wrote: "In the higher walks of intellectualism, this was the correct way to talk about Meredith before he went out of fashion. Personally, I don't believe a word of it. My soul requires that reality should be robust and recognizable."

––––––––

It remains to try to determine just what of Meredith's fiction merits recommendation to readers of the present time unfamiliar with his work. I have not addressed myself to his poetry because that has not fallen into the oblivion accorded to so many of his novels. Perhaps the harshest of Meredith's contemporary critics was his good friend Henry James, whose complaint about *Lord Ormont* has already been quoted. It is useful also to quote his much more laudatory assessment of Meredith, written in a letter to Edmund Gosse, three years after Meredith's death.

> Still, it abides with us, I think that Meredith was an admirable spirit even if not an *entire* mind; he throws out, to my sense, splendid great moral and ethical, what he himself would call "spiritual" lights, and has again and again big strong whiffs of manly tone and clear judgment. The fantastic and mannered in him were as nothing, I think, to the intimately sane and straight; just as the artist was nothing to the good citizen and liberalized bourgeois.

In this respect we recall that Meredith once wrote: "Many of the famous are only clever interpreters of the popular wishes. Real greatness must be based on morality" (Edel, ed., *Henry James' Letters*). Henry James was such a believer in his own concept of the tightly organized novel seen through carefully differentiated points of view that he sometimes failed to appreciate other literary devices. Percy Lubbock, his disciple, who understood James's methods as no other literary critic, was nonetheless sufficiently detached from the "master" to grasp the value in utterly different writers. He saw the greatness in Meredith, and quoting the latter's statement that "my characters are actual yet uncommon," he added that Meredith required a framework "florid and artificial" so that his characters "could not merely be themselves but strikingly and exceptionally themselves" (*The Craft of Fiction*).

Lubbock also wrote about Meredith's characters:

> In the later books the treatment is less biographic and more discursive; "what do they do?" gives place to "how did they come to do it?" The change of structure may be expressed by saying that the movement spreads outward from within, swaying from side to side into the recesses of the characters to be examined.

Oscar Wilde compared Meredith to Robert Browning in *The Critic as Artist*:

> Yes, Browning was great. And as what will he be remembered? As a poet? Ah, not as a poet! He will be remembered as a writer of fiction, as the most

supreme writer of fiction, it may be, that we ever had. His sense of dramatic situation was unrivalled, and, if he could not answer his own problems, he could at least put problems forth, and what more could an artist do? Considered from the point of view as a creator of character he ranks next to him who made Hamlet. Had he been articulate, he might have sat beside him. The only man who can touch the hem of his garment is George Meredith. Meredith is a prose Browning, and so is Browning. He used poetry as a medium for writing in prose.

I find the finest appreciation of Meredith's prose in Emile Legouis and Louis Cazamian's *History of English Literature* (1960):

He has the gift and feels the desire of precise, close, adequate knowledge; and the subject that he wants to know is man. But his analysis works by a series of visions and "élans"; it recreates its object much rather than it divides it. The most delicate shades of the moral world, like those of the visible landscape, caught with the sharpest perception, are not isolated by him; he at once allows them to melt with all the others into a changing play of shapes and colours, the moving fascination of which holds his gaze fast. A subtle psychologist, he is at the same time a lover of fancy and a poet. So keen is the eagerness that carries him to instantaneous notations, that he grants but very slight care to the indispensable connections of style; his art is that of an impressionist.

I think that the novel which to a reader new to Meredith would be the most satisfactory with which to begin is *The Egoist*. It is more like other Victorian novels in plot and treatment than anything else he wrote, and it offers little difficulty in theme or details. That it is a great novel I have already attempted to show. For a second reading I would suggest *Diana of the Crossways,* perhaps the fastest moving and most dramatic of the novels. By then the reader should be ready for *Beauchamp's Career,* which offers both what is best and most off-putting in Meredith to the uninitiated. After that he will either be through with Meredith or hooked. And if hooked he will read all the others, even including *The Amazing Marriage* and *One of Our Conquerors.* And he will enjoy a unique aesthetic experience.

Suggested Reading

Hammerton, J. A. *George Meredith in Anecdote and Criticism.* London: Grant Richards, 1909.

Jones, Mervyn. *The Amazing Victorian*. London: Constable, 1999.

Meredith, W. M., ed. *The Letters of George Meredith*. New York: Charles Scribner's Sons, 1912.

Priestly, J. B., *George Meredith*. New York: Macmillan, 1926.

Sassoon, Sigfried. *Meredith*. New York: Viking, 1948.

Shaheen, Mohammad. *George Meredith: A Reappraisal of His Novels*. London: Macmillan, 1981.

Stevenson, Lionel. *The Ordeal of George Meredith*. New York: Charles Scribner's Sons, 1953.

Williams, Joan. *Meredith: The Critical Heritage*. New York: Barnes & Noble, 1971.

About the Author

Louis Auchincloss is the author of sixty previous works of fiction and non-fiction, spanning seven decades from his first novel, *The Indifferent Children,* in 1947 to his most recent books, *The Scarlet Letters* and *East Side Story.* A former president of the American Academy of Arts and Letters, Auchincloss has been honored as a "living landmark" by the New York Landmarks Conservancy.